I Do Believe;
Help Me With My Unbelief!

My Journey Toward
Uncompromising Faith in God

Tammy Schaefer

I Do Believe; Help Me With My Unbelief!

This book is dedicated first of all to God, who gave me this message of hope to share with the world. It's dedicated to my husband Rick and daughter, Asia who survived the journey with me and loved me when I was completely unloveable. My pastor, Rick Evans, the first pastor I have ever met that honestly shared the mess he was and how God transformed him and continues to transform him. My good friends Holly and Barbara, who constantly challenge me to step into the greatness that God has called me to. J.R. Fisher, who helped me begin the healing process. My foster Mom, who loved me and adopted me into her heart as one of her own. My foster sister, Gail, who is the sister I was blessed to grow up with and who has inspired me to keep going even when it's difficult. My mother and father who did the best they could with what they knew. My sisters, who survived the loss of their big sister and now have welcomed her back into their lives. There are so many others that have made this book possible with prayers, encouragement and financial support. Michelle, Tammy & Jenny, of Everyday Lifeline, Tammy Osborne-Dieffenbach, Vicky, Carrie, Donna, Jean, Natalie, Carmela, Marie, and Stacie, and so many others that have blessed me in so many ways. Thank you to all of you!

Table of Contents

Introduction

The day that changed my life was a Sunday morning in 2010. I had been stumbling around in the dark, feeling defeated and alone. I had spent a large portion of my life trying to overcome the effects of emotional, physical and sexual abuse from my childhood. I wanted to believe that God loved me no matter what I had done.

My family and I had moved to Florida to make a fresh start and shortly after moving my husband was laid off from his job and had not been able to find another one. My daughter, who had been accepted into the Navy's nuclear program and had what we believed was an amazing future ahead of her, had been discharged because of a knee injury. I had watched helplessly as she fell into anger and despair over her shattered dream. I felt like we had been completely abandoned by God and could see no light at the end of the tunnel. Once again, I had checked out and become a victim of my circumstances.

I was at my lowest point that Sunday morning when I walked into church. For the first time in my life, I had no plan, no dream, and had decided I needed to be realistic and accept my lot in life. I was nobody special, and it was high time I started acting that way. Who was I to think I deserved to see my dreams become a reality?

My pastor began his message out of Mark 9: 23-24, "If you can?" said Jesus. "Everything is possible for him who believes." Immediately the boy's father exclaimed, "I do believe, help me overcome my unbelief!" He had my undivided attention at that moment. He continued to talk about how this man had struggled with his faith and had asked Jesus to help him. I had been beating myself up nearly all my life because of my lack of faith, and this felt like a life preserver thrown to me by the Holy Spirit.

I realized that it wasn't God who was condemning me for my lack of faith, but the enemy. I was sick and tired of being sick and tired and suddenly realized that I had tried everything except asking God to change me. That very day I began to plead with God to help me with my unbelief. You see, I knew God was there and I knew He performed mighty miracles for others, but I didn't think that He wanted to perform them for me. Who was I to think that God cared enough about me and my circumstances to ever move on my behalf? This was the beginning of the breakthrough that I had searched for in vain for many years. "I do believe; help me with my unbelief!"

Chapter 1

I was born into a family of broken people, as everyone is. I was born on Christmas Day and reminded every year how my mom missed a big turkey dinner because I was born. I allowed this to give me the belief that I was unwanted and unloved. I desired so much to be celebrated and feel special.

My parents were very poor when I was born. They were married two days before I was born. I was told by relatives that this was because my father didn't want to admit that he was my father for much of the time leading up to my birth. He was raised in a godly home, so I believe this was hard for him to admit. I'm sure this was devastating to my mother. She was just out of high school and her family was very disappointed in her. She must have believed she was all alone in the world and had no one.

I remember hearing stories of my parents making a bed for me out of dresser drawer because they had no money to buy me a crib. My mother worked days and my father worked nights, and he watched me during the day. Many times he would turn the TV on and put me in front of it, so he could get a few hours of sleep. When he woke up I was always there so he assumed that everything was as it should be.

One day however, when I was three he awoke a little earlier than usual and I was nowhere to be found. The front door was unlocked, the chain lock undone. He ran outside searching for me and saw our neighbor. My father asked him if he had seen me, and our neighbor said "Yes, she's just out making her rounds." He went on to explain that I would stop in at his house and get some crackers or cookies, and move along to the next house and so on until I had made my rounds around the neighborhood. I would eat everything, go back into our house, put the chain lock back in its place and be back in front of the TV before my father would awaken from his nap.

My father would tell this story constantly to people, always bragging about how smart I was. I never realized until much later how angry I felt every time he told this story. They left me alone to occupy myself a lot as a child. I believe that this along with other situations in my childhood is why I have always been such an independent person. I always had a strong belief that it was my responsibility to take care of myself, because nobody else was going to. I didn't believe God would take care of me, because I thought that was my job.

Some of the fondest memories of my childhood are from when we lived in Florida. We lived in the Tampa area from the time I was around one year old until I was almost five years old. I remember my grandfather taking me to the beach often. He had an incredible love for the ocean which he passed onto me. He taught me to swim and to be safe in the water. I remember one incident very clearly. He had taken me to the beach and I was swimming rather far from the shore. After what seemed like a short time he started waving me to come back into shore. I wasn't ready to go home and I tried to ignore him. He became very insistent. When I finally obeyed and came back to shore he told me that there were sharks circling not far from where I was swimming. I realize now that God had been watching over me.

Those times I spent with my grandfather at the ocean were probably one of the few times I ever felt really safe in my life. My grandfather and my father would sometimes take me out with them when they would go fishing in my grandfather's boat. The ocean has remained the place I go to be at peace. It's the place I feel that I'm truly connected with God.

I also remember spending time with my grandmother while she worked in her flower beds. It always seemed to give her great joy nurturing the plants. I remember she had the most beautiful rose bushes and azalea bushes I have ever seen. The smell of a rose still takes me back to that time. She also made homemade yogurt, and always seemed happy with the simple things in life. I always felt special and loved whenever I had the opportunity to be with my grandparents. My mom's brother, Uncle Melvin, used to bring me gifts and make me laugh a lot. He picked on me a lot, but I knew it was because he loved me. I always felt safe and happy when I spent time with them. I felt like I mattered to them.

One of my earliest negative memories is when I was three years old. I was playing with our Siamese cat, Ching Lee, in the yard. I was most likely tormenting him. My mom took him into the house and wouldn't allow me in. I believe her intention was to give the poor cat a break, but at three years old I didn't understand. All I remember was I wanted to go into the house, she wouldn't let me and how hurt and unloved I felt. I believed she cared more about the cat than she did about me.

I also remember running through our house one day. I kept running faster and faster through the archways that connected our living room and dining room, and then I woke up in the back seat of our car. I later found out that I had run into the corner of the wall and split my forehead open. My dad would tell this story on many occasions. He would always share how scared he was and that he couldn't stand to see the doctor sew my forehead closed again. Every time I heard him tell this story, I remember thinking how much he must have loved me.

Another strong memory I have is waking up one night in the darkness and I didn't know where I was. I started to cry out loudly and then my mom's voice came to me clearly in the darkness. She said, "You fell out of bed, just get back into bed." I really wanted her to come in, comfort me and tell me everything was going to be alright. My mother didn't seem to understand how frightened I was. I thought I just needed to stop being a baby and take care of myself.

Throughout my childhood, whenever these incidents would happen it strengthened the belief that no one was going to take care of me. I soon decided to stop asking for help, because it seemed that no one was going to help me anyway. There was a time that I woke up in the middle of the night frightened by a nightmare and my Aunt Janet came and comforted me. The next morning my parents scolded me for waking her up. I believed that I was not worth the trouble to be comforted. This belief made it so difficult to allow myself to be vulnerable to anyone and especially to God.

I remember how sad I was when we had to move from Florida to Pennsylvania. I was only four, almost five, but I remember not wanting to leave. I spent most of my life wishing I could move back to Florida. My father had decided we should go back to Pennsylvania and live with his parents. He didn't think he could make a decent living in Florida, so we moved back to Pennsylvania. He worked as a cook and went back to truck driving school at night.

We lived in the basement apartment of the house my grandfather had designed and built. I remember it seemed like a mansion to me. It had a stone archway in the front with a large R on it, which stood for the family name. There was a large front porch that ran the length of the house. Inside was a huge kitchen and living room. The living room had mirrors on one wall with gold designs in them. The walls were covered with gold wallpaper with raised blue felt designs. There were several bedrooms and bathrooms. My grandparents had 10 children and a few of them still lived with them. We lived with them for a time and then my mother and father were able to buy a trailer and rent a space in a trailer park.

Later we were able to move into a small apartment. Our landlord, Mr. Brandt and his wife were God-fearing people. It was Mrs. Brandt who first introduced me to the gospel. She held a small Good News Club in her home. She made sure to come and pick me up so I was able to attend. I remember the little book that told the story of Jesus. It had a black page that stood for our sins, the red page that stood for Jesus blood, the white page that stood for how Jesus blood washed our sins white as snow, the green page that stood for growing in Christ, and the gold page that stood for the streets in heaven paved with gold. The one thing I realized was that heaven was certainly a place I wanted to live in. I didn't ask Jesus into my heart then, but it certainly opened the door for God to start working on my heart. Eventually my parents were able to earn enough money to build our house. That took me away from Mrs. Brandt and the Good News Club, but I never forgot the things I learned there.

Chapter 2

During my younger years, my family spent a lot of time at my grandparents' home. We would go there once a week and play cards and other games. It was a happy time. My grandparents also had a second home in Tioga County, in the mountains. My grandmother would pick me up and take me up there to spend time with them over the summer. I felt loved by my grandparents, and they were very clear about their belief in God. I remember watching the 700 Club with my grandmother and hearing about God. My grandmother also taught me to crochet, knit and macramé. I enjoyed all these things. My grandfather made crafts out of wood, and would often allow me to join him. I enjoyed being with my grandparents and loved learning from them.

At home things were rather different. My relationship with my mother was very hard. She always worked full-time and had several part-time jobs, and so did my father. They both worked very hard to make a better life for us. When I was very young my dad would go out on the weekends and either work or do something for himself. My mother was often left at home alone with me, and I always believed that she resented it. There were a few times I remember when she was in a good mood. We listened to oldies on the radio, and sometimes we would dance together.

My relationship with my father was good. I was "Daddy's Girl" and he showered a lot of attention on me. I always looked up to my father because he had so much compassion for others. He stood firm on his beliefs whether it was popular to do so or not. He talked about his relationship with God often.

I remember vividly that we had a painting on the living room wall of a truck driver driving down the road and being led by Jesus. We also had a picture in the dining room of Jesus standing outside a door knocking. He was not shy about sharing Jesus with anyone. I thought of my father as a strong Christian and my hero. It seemed that he was the one I could approach, without fear of rejection, when I had a problem.

I remember one particular incident when I had procrastinated on a book report and project and was working on it past my bedtime. My mom got very angry with me and told me to go to bed. My dad came home from work a little while later and helped me make a really cool log cabin for my project. I felt like he was the one I could always count on to help me.

He always showed me affection, and I believed that he loved me much more than my mother did. As I got older he would take me along with him on the weekends when he would go out to my grandparents and mow their lawn, or he would go out and fly model airplanes, and we would go bike riding. He was always doing something. We usually watched Saturday morning cartoons and on Sundays we would watch the Marx Brothers and The Three Stooges together. Yes, I was certainly "Daddy's Girl".

I fondly remember one Christmas morning, I came out into the living room and there was a beautiful wooden desk and chair with a large red bow on it. My father stood beside it beaming at me, and I could tell that it pleased him so much to be giving me this gift.

My father had studied to earn his pilot's license to fly small engine planes and on his thirtieth birthday we had a birthday party for him at the airport. After the party we went up to fly in an airplane, and he let me fly for a while. I remember thinking that one day I was going to be a pilot, too. It felt so good flying up above everything, as if I was free from everything going on below.

My father also took me to see evangelists like Billy Graham and Jimmy Swaggart from time to time. Listening to them preach stirred up wonderful feelings inside of me. I wanted to know more about this God that they knew. I don't remember my mom ever being with us when we went to these revivals and I'm not sure if that was her choice or not. I didn't realize until much later that my mom and dad in many ways lived separate lives.

It always seemed that I was either spending time with my father or spending time with my mother. I don't remember spending much time together as a family, except Sundays for church and dinner. My mom almost always made a nice homemade dinner on Sunday afternoon. Sundays were usually good days in our house.

One weekend my mom and I spent baking and talking. I remember how good it felt to be doing something with her that was fun. During our conversation she told me not to ruin my life the way she had. She told me not to get married and have children young. She looked so sad when she said this to me. She didn't realize that I would internalize this and decide that I was the one who had ruined her life.

A short time later when I was going into bed one night, I gave my father a hug, which was my nightly custom, and he told my mother she needed to give me a hug. She gave me a cold mechanical hug that left me wishing she wouldn't have hugged me at all. I didn't understand until many years later that my mother felt so controlled by my father that she carried deep resentment as a result. She always seemed to direct her anger at me, and I thought I was doing something wrong. I now believe she felt trapped and unable to do anything to improve her life.

I worked hard to try to get my mother to accept me and be proud of me, not understanding that she viewed me as the reason her life was so hard. She was very volatile and unstable emotionally. She was physically and emotionally abusive, quick with complaints and criticism, and very rarely pointing out anything that I was doing right. At times she would get angry with me and not talk to me for days. It was as if I didn't exist. Other times she would become enraged and physically attack me. I lived in fear of making her angry.

The only time I remember her being happy was when she would play the piano. She would come alive when she sat at the piano and ran her fingers over the keys. I could've sat for hours listening to her play; it gave me such comfort.

She also helped me develop a strong love of musicals. We watched musicals together and no matter what else was going on at that time it didn't matter; at that moment I believed she loved me. I also loved listening to oldies on the radio, while we cleaned, or dancing to them on evenings when my father was working late.

Rock music was off-limits and I believe another way for my father to attempt to exercise his control over her. I have a strong love and appreciation of all types of music because of my mother sharing those times with me. She never knew how much I admired her and how much I wished I could be like her. She was so beautiful and seemed to be so successful in her work. She just seemed to be very unhappy most of the time. I realized many years later that she did not have a very happy childhood and she regretted being married so young. She felt like she had been cheated out of a good life.

I used to sneak into her bedroom when she was working. I would look at her makeup and jewelry, all the while, wishing that I could be as beautiful as she was. I always thought I was closer to finding out more about her when I looked at her things. She was so shut down emotionally, and I longed to know more about where she came from and how I could be like her. After several years she discovered that I had been looking through her things and she put a lock on her door. This was devastating to me because I knew I had disappointed her, but I also thought it meant the end of my opportunity to get to know her.

My father often talked about how much he wanted to have a boy. I know he didn't realize the impact those words had on me. I tried to be a tomboy, so he wouldn't need to have a son. I spent years trying to be the person I thought my parents wanted me to be. I thought if I could just be good enough they would love me.

My father made sure we went to church every Sunday. It was hard for me to understand the difference between what I learned in Sunday school and what went on in our home. I asked God into my heart on Easter Sunday at the age of 9. They taught about how Jesus died on the cross for our sins, and then rose again. I realized at that moment I was a sinner and asked Jesus to forgive all my sins and come into my heart. I was so excited, and when I got out to the car my mom was on a rampage because I was late coming out. This made her late to prepare lunch and being 9 years old, I didn't understand why this was such a big deal. I believed once again a monumental event in my life was not worthy of celebration. I was saved but really didn't understand how to have a relationship with God. I knew about God, but really didn't understand who He was for me. Something deep inside me told me there was more, but it would be many years until I was ready to give up my anger, my will and my belief that God couldn't use me.

My parents had another daughter when I was eight and then another when I was ten. Each time my mother was pregnant, my father would say he was hoping for a boy, but he ended up with three girls. I do remember times when he would say that God had a sense of humor, and he did feel blessed to have three beautiful girls.

My mother seemed to show them the affection I had so long craved. She seemed to put them up on a pedestal, and seemed to always give them priority. They were so much younger than I was and as a result of my jealousy, I never allowed myself to truly bond with them. I wanted them to love me, but holding onto all that resentment made that impossible. As the years went by, I felt less and less like I fit in with my family.

School was always an escape for me; it was a break from home. I enjoyed learning and the teachers always seemed to like me. I had a very difficult time making friends. My parents really never allowed me to be around children my own age, and it seemed like I had nothing in common with them when I did have an opportunity to be with them. My mom always worked at least two jobs and it often was expected that I should make dinner during the week. I remember thinking I was going to be like my mom when I grew up. She seemed so independent, loved and respected by so many people. I would come home from school do my chores, complete my homework, and start dinner. I believed that my needs for companionship and fun were not important. I felt so lonely most of the time. I resented my mother for not allowing me to have any after school activities, but I also admired her at the same time for being what I thought was an important person. It was very confusing for me.

I remember as I got older my mother would let me help her bake on the weekends. She would bake cookies, pies, and apple dumplings. To this day, when I smell an apple dumpling it brings back happy thoughts. During those times, just like when we watched musicals, I felt loved by her.

Chapter 3

At the age of twelve my parents enrolled me in a private Christian School. I learned a lot about the judgment of God and how unworthy I was to receive His love. I don't recall hearing anything about how God loved us while we were still sinners. I got the message that He died for my sins, so I had to spend my entire life paying Him back. I thought God expected us to suffer through this life until Jesus came back to take us to heaven. The more I learned the more condemned I felt. I thought that there was nothing I could do to make God happy with me.

They had bonfires to burn rock music albums. I remember one of my friends telling me that they told her she needed to burn her Air Supply records. Music was the one thing I had in common with my mother. Music made the time I spent alone bearable. I loved the Beatles, Buddy Holly, Simon and Garfunkel and many others. Now they were telling me that it was a sin to enjoy listening to this music. They taught us that all secular music was the devil's music. I couldn't understand how they could consider one of the special things that I enjoyed doing with my mother as a sin. It always made me worry that she was going to go to hell because she enjoyed that "devil music". I began to believe that God was someone who wanted to take away anything that I considered fun in my life. I believed that He just was waiting for me to mess up so He could punish me. I believed I would never be good enough to be loved by God or anyone else.

They showed us the movie "The Thief in the Night". I started to fear that Jesus was going to return and my mother was going to be left here on earth to suffer. It also planted a doubt in my mind about whether I was really saved or not. I remember waking up from a nap one afternoon, and my parents were gone. I went outside and the neighbors were gone. At that moment, I thought the rapture had taken place and I wasn't good enough to go to heaven. Later my parents came home and told me they hadn't wanted to wake me from my nap. I carried a lingering doubt after that about whether I was really bound for heaven. I was not able to overcome that fear for many years.

Around the same time my father started to show inappropriate affection towards me. He would ask me to give him massages and come into the bathroom to make sure I was bathing properly. My mother seemed to turn a blind eye, and even though I believed that it wasn't right, I didn't think I was allowed to say no. It seemed that the more attention my father gave to me, the angrier my mother was with me. I remember thinking there must be something wrong with me, that it was somehow my fault. I felt betrayed because my dad was the one I had always looked up to and I thought he was the one that would protect me. I was completely isolated and alone, my only friends were our pets and I became deeply attached to them. After all, animals were safe. They wouldn't abuse me or get angry with me or hit me.

I spent a lot of time alone reading in my room when I wasn't working around the house. I read Agatha Christie, Sir Arthur Conan Doyle, and others. I lived in a fantasy world most of the time. I envisioned myself as the person who was supposed to save everyone that was being abused. I was always the one who was going to solve the crime and save the day. The only time I felt safe was at night in my bed. I would listen to evangelists like Lester Roloff, and Billy Graham on the radio and dream that maybe someday I would be good enough for God to use me to do something amazing here on earth.

I didn't know how to make friends very easily and over the next few years I became even more isolated as my parents' abuse escalated. I did manage to reach out and make one friend who became my best friend. Her name was Tina, and she seemed to accept me just the way I was. She didn't make fun of me, or talk about me behind my back. I decided that I could trust her. When I turned fifteen my grandmother became gravely ill with cancer and died six months after being diagnosed. I was devastated by her death. Things always seemed better when she came from Florida to visit us. I always felt safe from abuse while she was in our home. I couldn't believe I would never be able to see her again. She was one of the people that treated me like I was special and loved. Her death sent my mother further into herself and increased the attention my father paid to me. He started to come into my bed at night, and that was the end of my safe place.

Ever since I could remember, I had struggled with thoughts of suicide. One day I went into my mom and dad's room and took out the handgun my dad had stored in his night stand. I had decided to shoot myself. God was with me, even though I didn't know it at the time, and I couldn't bring myself to pull the trigger. I told myself that I was such a loser because I didn't even have the guts to kill myself. From that point on I thought about killing myself almost every day. It would be over two decades before the desire to end my life was gone forever.

At this point, I became increasingly withdrawn and my best friend Tina cornered me one day and refused to let me leave until I told her what was bothering me. I told her about my father's abuse and she immediately said I needed to tell someone. She told me what I had known in my heart all along, that this was not right. I was horrified at the thought of telling this horrible secret, but I knew it would not stop unless I did something about it. I also realized that if I didn't speak up there would be no one to protect my sisters and my father would probably not stop with me.

Tina went with me when I told my favorite teacher, Mrs. Graeff, who then took me to our principal. As my story started to come out, they invited the church's pastor and lawyer to become involved. It soon became all too clear that they didn't believe what I was telling them and that they were worried about the school's reputation. They wanted me to go home and tell my mother, but I was terrified of what she might do to me. I refused to go home, and eventually, they called my mother and father to come and meet them at the school. I was hoping to be gone before they got there, but they were coming in the front as Mrs. Graeff and I were leaving. I will never forget the look my mother gave me as she was coming in the front of the school. She was projecting such anger toward me; I believed she would have beaten me to a pulp if she had been able to get her hands on me.

While they had their meeting at the school, Mrs. Graeff, took me to our family doctor to have a physical exam. She was told that she had to wait in the waiting room and I had to go into the exam room all by myself. When the doctor came in, he started to question me about what had happened. I remember he kept saying, "This can't be true, I know your mother." I thought what does knowing my mom have to do with my father abusing me? He asked me if I could be pregnant. He said that if I was pregnant I needed to have an abortion. I was horrified! Didn't he know that having an abortion was a sin? He told me that the baby would be deformed, and it would be cruel to bring a baby into the world that would have so many problems. Then he asked me how I expected to raise a baby on my own. I was so scared; I just kept thinking that this must be a punishment from God. He ordered a pregnancy test and then examined me. The pregnancy test was negative, and the exam showed no substantial proof of the abuse.

That night I went home with Mrs. Graeff and her husband. I stayed with them for a week. I really enjoyed staying with them; things seemed so calm in their home. I found myself wishing that they could be my family. After one week, I was told I needed to stay with another teacher, Mrs. Morris. I stayed with her and her husband for a week as well. At the end of that week, I was told that my parents were taking me out of the school and I was sent to live with my paternal grandparents.

Chapter 4

I spent about three months with them and was told I was ruining everyone's lives. My grandmother tried to convince me to change my story. She asked me one time why I was doing this. I told her I had to tell the truth to help save my sisters. She said that if I really wanted to save my sisters I should have stayed there so I could protect them from my dad. At that moment, I believed that I had made a big mistake by speaking out about my father's abuse. I told myself I was bad and was ruining my family's life. I thought this was a punishment from God for all the things I had done wrong. I wanted someone to take my side and protect me.

Most of the time I spent with my grandparents is a blur. I remember my parents coming over to visit occasionally. They would take me into the living room and plead with me to "stop lying" so that I could go back home with them again. They told me that if I would only change my story I could redecorate my room and have that pet rabbit I had always wanted. After these interrogations they would leave and my grandmother would ask me questions and try to convince me to change my story. I didn't find out until many years later that my grandmother had protected my aunts from my grandfather by telling them to put their dressers in front of their bedroom door at night so my grandfather couldn't get in. This was the way her generation believed that these things should be handled. This was the dark family secret that no one talked about.

I realize now how the Holy Spirit was taking charge during this time. I wanted to change my story and go back home, but now I know it was the Holy Spirit in me that kept me from doing that. So many people have told me over the years that I was so brave and courageous. I didn't feel any of those things. I was a terrified fifteen year old child, who believed she had just ruined her life and the lives of her whole family. That was exactly what the devil wanted me to think and he did get his way for many years. God has recently revealed to me that this was at the root of why I believed that I always ruined everything in my life. I always assumed if something was wrong that it was my fault. I've always felt that I didn't deserve to have any good things in my life. Whenever something good did happen I worried about when it would all go wrong. I never allowed myself to enjoy anything for fear that it would be taken away.

In addition to leaving home, I had to go from a private school to a large public school. I wasn't able to see my friend Tina anymore. Her parents would not allow her to have contact with me. I was the bad seed and she needed to be protected from me. I didn't know how to connect with anyone at my new school and was really afraid to even try. My grades went downhill and I went from an almost all A student to failing Algebra. I was devastated but I just didn't know how to concentrate.

In addition to my grades dropping, I was forced to deal with bullies. I lived with the threat of being beaten up on a daily basis. I felt so alone and thought that no one would ever be able to understand what I was going through.

On some level, I believed I deserved what was happening to me. I believed I was being punished for standing up against my parents. The devil kept bringing to my mind Exodus 20:12 "Honor your father and mother…" I thought that God was punishing me because I was not honoring them but instead getting them in trouble and making their life so hard. I really thought that this was entirely my fault.

My parents and I saw a counselor a few times. I remember on our last visit she told my dad that even if I was lying that there was something that they were doing to cause me to lie. My father was outraged and that was the last time we saw that counselor.

They finally realized that I wasn't going to change my story and they checked me into the hospital to have a series of neurological tests done. My grandmother told me that I was either hallucinating or making this story up. I remember hoping that the doctors would find something wrong with me. I didn't want to believe the truth. I wanted to be able to go back home. I was so afraid of what the future was going to bring.

The nurses, doctors, and counselors spent a few days running CAT scans, blood work, and psychological tests on me, and finally came to the conclusion that I needed to be protected from my family. They began to search for a foster home I could be placed in. I had to stay in the hospital for a week until they found a safe home for me.

I have often looked back at this time in my life and compared myself to Joseph. He was taken away from his family and sold into slavery. I was taken away from my family and placed somewhere completely new. Unlike Joseph, I chose to become angry and blame God. I have not read anything in the Bible that says Joseph expressed anger at God or his family. He always prospered in every situation that God placed him in. In fact, at the first opportunity, he went out of his way to let his family know that they were forgiven, and that God had used them to do something bigger with his life. This is incredibly humbling to me. I have often wished that I would've chosen to walk in love and forgiveness, instead of anger and bitterness. Recently God revealed to me that He used me and this situation to shed light on the generational curse of abuse in the family. It was broken with me. I love that God says the sins of the father will flow down into the third and fourth generation, but the blessings flow down through a thousand generations. That is a source of great comfort to me.

After my week in the hospital, I was told that they had found a wonderful new family for me to live with. I was happy to be leaving the hospital, but scared by the prospect of moving in with people I didn't know. What if they didn't like me? What if they wanted to hurt me?

Chapter 5

I remember meeting my foster mom for the first time. She was so nice, and I believed that finally I would find the love and acceptance that always seemed to be missing in my life. She told me that I could call her Mom if I wanted to. My own mother would not allow me to call her mom; she always told me to call her Mother. This always seemed so cold and formal to me. The first week with this new family was so hard. I missed my sisters and was afraid of what was happening to them. I felt like I was in a dream and any day I would wake up and realize that I was back at home. My foster home was safe, and my foster mother was a loving woman, but the only thing I allowed myself to think about was what I had lost.

My father had forced me to save every bit of money I received as gifts from others over the years, and it totaled somewhere between $600 - $700 dollars. After I was placed in my foster home, I went to close my account and discovered that my parents had already closed it. When I questioned them about it, they told me that it was payment for all the pain and suffering I had caused them. At that moment I decided it wasn't safe to save money. They also fought the courts and said that they could not afford to pay support for me. I was told by my court appointed lawyer that they said they didn't make enough money to pay to take care of me. I decided that this meant that I wasn't worth enough to be taken care of. These lies would plague me throughout my adult years, making it impossible to manage my money wisely or to trust God with my finances.

My foster mom was so kind to me and she worked hard to help me adjust to living in my new environment, but all I wanted was for my family to take me back and love me. My anger and belief that I was unwanted and unloved was directed at my foster family, because after all, they were there. I was so miserable, but could not break away from the fear of the rejection I thought was inevitable. I believed that if I really allowed them into my heart they would only reject me, and decided I wasn't going to allow myself to be rejected by anyone ever again. It was nearly two decades before I would allow myself to trust anyone.

My foster mom and father had several children. There was Gail, who was a year younger than me. There was Kerry who was a few years older than I was. He was the big brother I'd never had. There was another sister, Kristi and her husband Barry. Kristi and Barry were like a really cool aunt and uncle to me. Gail and I would spend a lot of time with them over the years that I lived in the foster home. Then there was Little Denny, who was called Little Denny, because my foster father was Big Denny. Little Denny was around 5 years old when I came to live with them. He was one of the most ornery little boys I had ever met, but he stole my heart with his mischievous smile. Then there was Cathy, the little girl that my foster parents had adopted. She had come from a very abusive home. She was several years younger than I was, and we just never seemed to become close.

Gail shared her bedroom with me. She had a bunk bed and I thought it was really cool to share a room and to have a sister who was closer to my age. This lasted for about a week and then it ceased to be fun for me. She always wanted to be on the top bunk. If she wanted to have the light on, it stayed on, regardless of whether or not I wanted to sleep. She was in charge and I certainly resented her for it. She would go to visit her father sometimes, and get special gifts from him. When she came home I resented her for getting what I thought was special treatment.

I didn't get any gifts when I saw my parents. In fact, the first few visits I had with my parents were very stressful. We had to meet at the children's services building and my parents refused to bring my sisters along with them. My caseworker had to go to court and fight for my right to be able to visit with my sisters. My parents finally agreed to visits in their home. When my caseworker and I visited with them my father was usually drunk. He sat in the kitchen reading the Sunday comics and ignoring me. My sisters sat on the loveseat in the living room with my mom. I had to carry the conversation most of the time. My sisters huddled next to my mother, and seemed terrified. I found out years later that my parents had told my sisters that they had to be careful or I was going to take them away with me.

Gail and I fought constantly, just like real sisters tend to do. This was very strange to me; I thought she hated me. I wanted her to love me but didn't know how to break through that wall of anger. The family seemed to love and care for each other so much. I wanted that more than anything but with my fear of rejection I wouldn't allow myself to be vulnerable again. They did things very differently from the way my family had done them and in the beginning I just thought they were very strange. At the same time, I wanted to be allowed into their lives. It was a very confusing time for me. I wouldn't allow them to get to know the real me for a long time.

I started counseling with an abuse counselor shortly after I moved in with them. I sat in the counselor's office and told her that I was fine. By that time I had suppressed my feelings of anger and I didn't understand why everyone thought I needed help. After all, this whole situation was entirely my fault. It didn't take long for everyone to realize that the counseling wasn't having the effect that it should.

I stopped attending counseling and started attending a support group for sexually abused girls, where I met other girls like me. It seemed that all the other girls had been abused so much worse than I had been, and I started to believe that I had no right to feel like I was abused. I reasoned that my abuse wasn't really that bad.

I began to brag about how wonderful my father was to anyone who would listen. I had a fantasy that he was going to come and apologize for everything he had done and take me back home. This seemed to infuriate my foster mom; she just could not understand how I could talk this way about my father. I was treating them so badly, and all she was trying to do was love me.

Then one day, I came downstairs in a rampage and announced to my mom that I was calling my caseworker so she could send me to a new home. She looked at me and said, "I already called her and you'll be leaving tomorrow." I was devastated! Why didn't anyone love me? I went up into the bedroom and cried for about an hour. If I was going to leave I wanted it to be on my terms. I wanted to be the one who rejected them, not the other way around. I decided that I didn't want to leave because I didn't want to go somewhere new and start all over again. Deep down in my heart I knew this family cared for me. I went downstairs, and tried to be as sweet as I knew how to be for the rest of the day. At the end of the day, I asked mom if she would let me stay. She told me that I could stay if I really wanted to. That was the first time in my life that I felt like I could be part of a family and really belong.

Over the next few years I became a part of the family but I still felt like I didn't deserve to belong. Gail and I did so many things together and I look back on those times now and realize that she was the sister I never thought I had.

We lived on a small farm in an old farmhouse and there was a barn out back. Gail and I used to go out and do aerobics to the Flash Dance and Footloose movie soundtracks. We went out there and danced around in our leotards, legwarmers and nylons (yes, it was the 80s).

Gail had her own TV. It seemed like such a luxury to have a TV in our bedroom. We would watch horror movies and stay up late and watch MTV on Friday nights. We loved to watch all of our favorite bands' music videos. One of our favorite programs to watch was Love Connection. I never realized until many years later all the wonderful memories we were making.

When Gail turned fifteen she really wanted to learn how to drive. Big Denny had a big orange LTD. When mom and he went out somewhere Gail pressured me into going out driving with her. She would mark the exact location of the car on the driveway with small twigs so that no one would know that it was moved. We would go out driving for a little while and stop by the local gas station and put a few dollars of gas into the tank.

One day while we were driving down the road we thought we saw mom and Big Denny coming the other way. We both ducked behind the dashboard, and then couldn't stop laughing when we realized that the orange LTD would be a big giveaway. Whenever Gail and I get together, this is always one of those times we reminisce about with hearty laughter.

Once a year, we would head out as a family on a vacation. They didn't have a lot of money but they always made vacation special. One of my favorite times was when we went to Ocean City, MD and rented a house. It had a dock on the back and Gail and I would spend nearly half the day catching blue crabs off the dock. We would bring them in and steam them in a big pot with Old Bay seasoning and spend the evening with our little mallets eating, talking and laughing with each other. We played cards, went for walks, and went to the beach; I remember wishing we could live there forever.

Another fun thing we did was sell sweet corn at the local Turkey Hill. Big Denny would plant a huge field of sweet corn and in the summer we would go out and pick enough to fill his pickup truck bed. He drove us out to the local Turkey Hill and we would stay out in the parking lot all day until we sold it all. He allowed us to keep the money we made for ourselves. It felt so good to be able to have some of my own spending money.

One year, Gail and I were allowed to each adopt a wild horse. Gail got a horse and named him Apache. I got one I named Sabrina. Neither one of us weighed enough to break our horses. Gail was given the opportunity to have a horse trainer come in to help her break Apache. She did ride him a lot. We could not afford to pay for a trainer for Sabrina, so we eventually had to find another home for her.

I used to try to ride Apache but it didn't work out very well. He certainly had a mind of his own. One day I was riding him down by the pasture, where our gelding pony stayed during the day. He came running up to the fence when I came by with Apache. Apache took off like a shot and ran through the trees in our back yard and I fell off. Another time I was riding him, and he saw Gail walking by the house. He took off running towards her. He ran up to my mom's clothes line, put his head down, and I went flying out over the top of his head. I hit the cement sewage cover that was lying on the ground. Gail ran over, looked at me, and ran off to bring Apache back to the barn. Everyone had a big laugh over that one. I didn't think it was funny at the time, but looking back now, it's another fond memory.

One year we planned a trip to Great Adventure in New Jersey with Kristi and Barry. We headed out on our journey in two separate cars. About an hour down the highway I had to use the bathroom so badly that I thought I was going to burst. Gail and I were in the car with Kristi and Barry and we were following mom and didn't know how to get there ourselves. One of us decided to take a piece of paper and write a large P on it. Mom didn't understand what we were trying to say. A cell phone would've solved this little problem but back then not many people had cell phones. Besides, if we had had a cell phone I wouldn't have this fond memory. We kept pointing to the big P, but to no avail. Needless to say I survived, but to this day I always set up a plan ahead of time for bathroom breaks whenever I'm on a trip.

I also remember the time when Kristi and Barry actually had a birthday party for me. It was the first time anyone had gone out of their way to celebrate my birthday. They gave me this beautiful gray cat as a gift. I named him Smokey. We took him home but he ran off a few days later and we never found him, but I couldn't forget how nice it was to finally have my birthday celebrated. I look back now at all these memories and wonder why I couldn't see how much they all loved me.

Mom decided to get a family picture taken of all her children. Instead of including me in the picture she decided that we would go to Hardees as a special treat. I know now that she didn't realize what this meant to me. I thought she was saying I wasn't really one of her children. This hurt very deeply, but we were able to clear the air a few years later.

We were able to make a special memory of our own. While we were sitting at the table eating at Hardees, a man walked in the door and blurted out something in Chinese. Mom and I looked at each other and burst out laughing. Unfortunately, I had just swallowed a large mouthful of soda and mom got a shower of soda all over her face and hair. To this day, whenever we see each other, we always have a hearty laugh about the soda shower.

I also enjoyed my brothers, Kerry and Little Denny. They are still both so special to my heart. Kerry always had a way of making me laugh no matter how down I was feeling. Little Denny was all little boy. He would give you this devilish smile and you couldn't stay mad at him no matter what he'd done. Kerry and Little Denny have both grown into extraordinary men. They are still very special to me.

I have so many precious memories of my foster family, and it still amazes me that I didn't realize what a gift God had given me by placing me in their home. Looking back now, I see how God was moving in my life and how He gave me the ability to love and be loved by this wonderful family.

I lived with them until I graduated from high school. I had really checked out on school while I was in the foster home. I didn't care about my grades anymore and just wanted everyone to leave me alone. I thought about joining the Air force after graduation, but of few of my friends told me it would be too hard and I decided I didn't want to be rejected so I didn't even try pursuing it. My state appointed caseworker and others around me kept saying I needed to have a plan for my life. I didn't care. I didn't have a clue who I was or what I wanted. I just wanted to graduate from high school and go somewhere where no one would tell me what I could or couldn't do. I wanted to be my own boss, and live life on my own terms. The problem was I didn't know what my terms were, and had no real plan. I finally told everyone to leave me alone. I decided to get a job and find a place to live.

Chapter 6

Upon graduation, I got a job at a fast food place and rented a room from a family friend. I spent most of the next year working, and living in a dream world. I thought if I could only find my Prince Charming, then life would be wonderful.

At nineteen, I met the man that I was to have my first significant relationship with. Craving unconditional love, I ignored all the warning signs. He was controlling, angry and cheated on me, and I chose to remain in the dark. In the beginning, he was so nice and caring. He made me feel special and wanted like never before. I wanted to be in a relationship so badly that I turned a blind eye to anything that I didn't want to see. We were both so young and in so much pain that we couldn't love each other. We didn't even know how to love ourselves. Honestly we brought out the worst in each other. We lived together for around three years and then we decided to live apart for a time and continued to date. Gail and I had recently been reunited so we decided to get an apartment together.

On July Fourth, my boyfriend and I had decided to go and see fireworks. It began to rain early in the day so he called me and said that he wanted to cancel our date. I insisted that we still get together, so he picked me up and we drove over to his mother's house. After a time, I noticed he had been gone for a while, and his mother seemed to be acting a little strange. I went to search for him and found him on the phone trying to cancel a date with another woman. I couldn't ignore the fact that he was cheating on me anymore. Eventually, we decided that we shouldn't see each other anymore.

After this, I chose to become extremely self-destructive. I became extremely promiscuous and did anything I could to get a man's, any man's, attention. I checked out and stopped caring about anyone but myself. I became a loser magnet. Any man who was within a ten mile radius of me who would abuse me was the man I would fall completely in love with and then cry "poor me" when the inevitable abuse began. I decided I wasn't worthy to be loved or worth waiting for and I had sex with anyone who would give me the opportunity. I self-medicated with alcohol and drugs, and stopped taking care of myself at all. I rarely had to pay for the drinks or the drugs; there was always a man more than willing to get me drunk or stoned. The price was my dignity most of the time. Of course, this was just another way for me to try and kill myself.

Gail and I did have a lot of fun living together again. We would stay up late and watch Love Connection together, while stuffing ourselves with Oreos. We lived across the street from a bar and restaurant and would spend some time over there as well. I lived with Gail for about a year. We worked and partied and things seemed good for a while. I really didn't do my part to help take care of the apartment. Our relationship was starting to deteriorate under the strain of my self-centered attitude and the extreme hatred I had for myself.

One day it was raining heavily and I got into my car to go to work. I realized my windshield wipers were not working but decided I couldn't miss work. I ran into a telephone pole as a result of not being able to see through the windshield.

A friend offered to help me get another car and I found another one for a few hundred dollars. That one lasted a couple of months, until someone ran me off the road. Then I was able to get another one for a couple hundred dollars. This one lasted me for a few months until I pulled out in front of someone at an intersection and that was the end of that car. I'd had three car accidents in the course of one year. Then I found out that I had no car insurance at the time of the last accident. I had sent my payment in late and they had decided to drop me. I decided to blame everyone else for my choices and built up great resentment at my circumstances. Why did all these bad things always happen to me? I decided to have a big pity party for myself once again. That was the end of my car and because I had no car insurance and no money saved I wasn't able to buy another one. Gail and I weren't getting along very well anymore because I was choosing not to take responsibility for my actions. I finally decided to move into the city so I would be able to use public transportation to get back and forth to work.

A friend had offered me a room in her apartment, so I moved in. I continued down my self-destructive path of partying and just doing whatever I could do to forget about the pain I was causing in my life. I had one really close friend at this point and we would go out drinking together all the time.

One night I called her, and asked her to come out with me. She said she couldn't because she had her children that weekend. They were young and really shouldn't have been left home alone. I wouldn't leave her alone until I had convinced her to leave them at home alone after they fell asleep and come party with me. She agreed and we went out to the bar. They woke up while she was away and the police were called. As a result, she ended up having a custody battle over her children. My thinking was so messed-up at the time. I didn't realize what an irresponsible thing this was, until a few years later when I had my own child.

On New Year's Eve, my ex-boyfriend showed up on my door step. I was so lonely and so was he so we decided we should get back together. I decided I wanted to have a baby with him. I thought that having a baby would make our relationship strong. Did I mention that my thinking was messed-up at that time? We tried for a couple months and then I got pregnant with my daughter, Asia.

Being pregnant filled me with an irresistible need to reconnect with my biological family. I believed I had to fix things with them. I wanted to get to know my sisters, and wanted them to be in my child's life. Going back home brought back all the unresolved feelings I had shoved down over the years. I became that young girl who wanted to be loved again. I began to get to know my sisters for the first time in my life. They were struggling with problems of their own at the time. My father was drinking a lot and the family was completely falling apart. The illusion of the perfect family was over. I spent a lot of time getting to know the sisters I had lost years earlier. I thought that we could be a family again. Meanwhile, I tried to be the good girl and get back in good standing with my father. I felt like I had a split personality. I loved him and wanted him to accept me but I was also angry at him and my mother. I wanted them to admit that they were wrong and tell me they were sorry. I wanted us to be a big happy family. I tried to pretend that the abuse had not taken place.

At the same time, I talked to my sisters and told them my truth about what had happened. I realize now, that I wanted my sisters to take my side. I didn't realize how unfair that was. I allowed myself to become very bitter over not being able to grow up with them. I expected them to welcome me with open arms, and respect me for having saved them from the abuse I had suffered. I didn't understand until many years later, that they couldn't possibly understand what I had been through. Their path was different and they had suffered their own abuse as a result of the aftermath of our family being fractured. I was also trying to maintain a relationship with my foster family at the same time and feeling misunderstood because my mom didn't seem to understand why I was trying to have a relationship with my biological family again. I didn't even try to understand why this would be so hard for her. I didn't care about anyone but myself.

Chapter 7

Having my daughter, Asia, was the most wonderful experience of my life but it also unleashed a tremendous rage I didn't even know was in me. When I gave birth to her, I began to really judge my parents for the way they had raised me. I could no longer pretend that the abuse hadn't happened. I set out to give her all the love and support I'd never had, but since I had turned my back on God, I couldn't teach her about having a relationship with God. I decided to play god and be the "perfect" mom. I had no idea what I was doing.

Asia's father and I lived with his father and step-mother after Asia was born. The day we brought her home from the Hospital he proposed to me. I thought we would get married and live happily ever after. We started fighting all the time because I resented him for spending so much time working. I was left alone with his step-mother and we didn't get along well. I had no car and felt trapped there every evening. After Asia was born it seemed like he couldn't stand to be around me anymore. We were able to buy a trailer and moved to my hometown when Asia was nine months old. I thought that since we finally had our own place we would be happy but things only seemed to get worse. We played house and I proceeded to blame him for my unhappiness.

One day my mom called me and told me that Gail had been in a bad accident. She said she was alive but badly injured and in intensive care. I immediately got ready and went to see her in the hospital. I went in to her room and thought I was in a nightmare. Her face was so badly damaged that I thought for a moment it just couldn't be her. I remember thinking I needed her to stay alive; I needed her in my life. I wasn't ready to lose her. She had my heart and the thought of losing her was unbearable.

We had been through so much together. We were even pregnant at the same time. She had a boy a few months after Asia was born. It made me realize that my foster family was too important to me to lose and I needed to make time to stay connected with them.

I started taking steps to be connected with them again. Gail went through a lot to recover from her injuries. She was able to go home from the hospital within three weeks but she had to have several surgeries and physical therapy. I was just so happy that she had survived. I know that God's hand was in it. She had fallen asleep behind the wheel and ran into a dump truck head on. When I saw the pictures, I knew she wouldn't have survived without God. It was a wakeup call for me but I didn't take advantage of it. I still didn't attempt to seek God.

I kept pressuring Asia's dad to set a wedding date and he refused. He continued to become more and more controlling and started to become abusive. I found myself trying to start fights and daring him to hit me. I couldn't understand why I was acting this way. I started to think that I deserved to be abused.

We were driving home from a visit with my foster family one Sunday afternoon, and he began to accuse me of flirting with one of my foster sister's boyfriends. I mocked him and he punched me in the face while we were still driving. I spent the rest of the ride home deciding how I was going to get my daughter out of the car and get away from him. We pulled in front of the house and I grabbed her out of the car seat. I went to a neighbor and called my mother, who lived only a few miles away. Asia's father became enraged and took the diaper bag into the house and wouldn't allow me to have it.

My mother and sisters came to pick me up and Asia and I went to stay with my family in their home. It was very hard to stay in the house where I had grown up and felt so abused. My father kept saying that he was going to have a talk with Asia's father and set him straight. In the end, he didn't do anything and I felt betrayed all over again. I thought that I had to stand alone and take care of this myself.

The next day, Asia's father came to talk to me. He said he was so sorry and pleaded with me to come back home. He promised he would go to counseling with me so we could work things out and make them better. We went to a counselor the next day and Asia and I moved back in with him. We attended counseling together twice and then he refused to continue.

A few weeks after Asia and I went back to live with him, his sister, Tina, confided to me that her husband was beating her. She swore me to secrecy, and I kept her secret. A few weeks later he murdered her. I blamed myself for her death.

At the time of her death, she had three young children. Asia's father said he wanted to marry me and asked me to help him raise Tina's two youngest children. They were three months and one and a half years old, and Asia was two. I decided it was my duty to take care of the two youngest, Alex and Cameron, after all, I thought it was my fault Tina was dead. I thought I was finally going to have the family I had always dreamed about. I set out to be the world's best mom and did what I could to provide a loving home for them.

Asia's dad began to take anti-depressants after his sister's death and his behavior became increasingly erratic. During the winter I awoke one morning and discovered that we had no heat. I talked to Asia's father and realized he had not paid the electric bill. I told him I needed to know what was going on and he told me the bills were none of my business. He had reasoned that because I wasn't working, I had no right to know what was going on with our finances. He kept all the bills and financial information locked up in a fire safe and I didn't know how much money he made or how it was being spent.

He became more and more controlling and started to become abusive as a result of the medication he was taking. I was not sleeping because I lived in constant fear that Tina's husband would come back to kill me and the children. He had taken off after they found her body and nobody knew where he was. I had constant vivid nightmares of waking up and finding the children dead. I wasn't able to sleep and wasn't eating properly. Things became so much worse and I finally knew I had to leave and decided that no one could take care of me and my daughter but me. My pride reared its ugly head once again. I carried great guilt for a long time because I was not able to take care of Tina's two babies but I knew I had to give my daughter a safe place to live.

I had become close to my Aunt Sis during this time. We were on a bowling league together and saw each other once a week. My aunt encouraged me to make some changes in my life for Asia's sake. She had watched me falter and punish myself for not being able to save Tina or take care of her children. She offered to let Asia and me stay with her until I could get on my feet.

We lived with her for about a month but I was so selfish and self-absorbed that she finally told me I had to leave. Thinking I had nowhere else to go, I asked Asia's father if I could come back. He agreed to let me move back in.

During the year I spent living with Asia's father, I began having feelings for a young teenage boy I had met. He gave me the attention I had been craving for so long. He told me how beautiful and young looking I was. No one had told me I was beautiful in quite some time. I found myself starting to develop strong feelings for him. His mother was a strong Christian woman and she began to notice something was off about our relationship. She stepped in and kept her son from spending time with me. I didn't realize how dangerous this relationship was. This was very painful and embarrassing for me but I know that it was God protecting me from doing something I would've regretted for the rest of my life. He prevented me from abusing someone the way I had been abused.

I spent much of that time becoming angrier with God. I blamed Him for Tina's death. I couldn't understand why he would have allowed her to die and me to live. I thought if anyone deserved to die it was me. I had made so many reckless decisions in my life and yet I was the one that survived. It didn't make any sense to me.

I spent that year working part-time at a local grocery store until I was able to save enough money to buy my own car. Asia's father was very upset when he realized that I had gone behind his back and bought a car and was also able to find a full-time job. He told me that I had to find a new place to live. A few days later I found an apartment for Asia and me to live in.

Chapter 8

Once I moved out, Asia went back and forth between her father's house and mine. He kept pleading with me to come back. He told me that I would never make it on my own. He didn't know this only strengthened my resolve to make it without him. I was so determined to make it on my own but I started right back into my self-destructive behavior.

On the weekends Asia was at her father's, I would go out drinking and smoking pot. All I had to do was go out to a bar and somebody would buy me a drink and they almost always had pot. It was so easy; I didn't even have to pay to feed my habit.

I also started a relationship with a man who would stop by to see me when he didn't have anything better to do. I knew he didn't care about me, so naturally I was madly in love with him. I spent several months working a full-time job and a part-time job trying to make enough money to pay the bills. I was also partying whenever I didn't work or have Asia. Sleep was something I thought I could do without.

During the summer my sister Terri and her friend Sherri would babysit Asia for me. After the summer, Terri had to go back to school and I had to take Asia to a babysitter that I didn't feel right about. She was the only one I could afford. Asia would cry every time I left her there, and when I would call to check on her, the babysitter would get angry with me. I felt paralyzed and completely helpless to change my situation.

I continued to punish myself for not being able to save Tina and for being a total failure at life. I decided it was my fault that my relationship with Asia's father hadn't worked out. I thought I had failed as a mother. I had no dreams and felt completely unworthy to have a life of abundance. I was just trying to check out of life. The emotional pain I felt was so unbearable that I often wished that God would end my life.

At this time, I started to connect with my sisters again. I felt like I had a chance at a second childhood and wanted them to treat me like a sister. I was struggling to support myself and Asia. At the same time, my parents had decided to get a divorce. My mother offered to allow Asia and me to come live with her. I thought I could help her save the house by living there and paying rent. I dreamed that my mom would finally be able to love me.

It was very strange living in the house where I had grown up. It brought back so many memories. I wanted all the years I had lost with my sisters back. I wanted my mom to welcome me back with open arms. I wanted my sisters to treat me like the sister I wanted to be. It was so hard for me to realize that life had gone on for them after I had left. They had to learn how to adjust to a life without me in it for so many years and I wanted them to treat me as if I had never left. I felt cheated out of my life. I was trying to earn their love, and got angry with them when they didn't seem to reciprocate the feelings I had. I couldn't understand why they didn't respect me for everything I had suffered to save them. I lived with them for about a year until my mom decided she wasn't going to be able to keep the house.

I met my husband around the same time. Rick and I met at my full-time job. I thought he hated me; he always looked so serious at work. Gail and I went out drinking one Friday night when Asia was with her father. We walked into the bar and Rick was there. I asked him to dance and we spent the rest of the night together. He came home with me and we just stayed up all night and talked. I couldn't believe there was a man who actually wanted to hang out and talk with me without having an ulterior motive.

We were only dating for a short time when he took me to meet his family. They were such wonderful people and I thought this was a family that could love me. When I met his grandmother for the first time she said to me, "Don't let my grandson live in sin with you." This scared me, because I knew how much his family meant to him. I was afraid to disappoint them. I cared for him so much but also was afraid that this was all just a trick. I thought if I stayed with him long enough he would start to treat me badly, just like I thought everyone else had in my life. I was terrified, so I broke up with him.

A few weeks later, he came back and asked me to go out with him again. I agreed and we started seeing each other again. During this time, I became very sick. The doctor's finally discovered that I had diseased tonsils and that they needed to be removed. The thought of having surgery terrified me but I knew that I couldn't go on the way I was going. Rick pampered me by taking me to a nice hotel the night before and then accompanied me to the hospital. When I came out of surgery I was so sick. He stayed in the waiting room the entire time and then comforted me through my recovery. He was holding my head up and holding my hair back while I was sick and I remember thinking he must really love me. I couldn't believe he would stay with me the entire time. It was the first time in my life I had received that kind of support. I thought, "This one's a keeper."

A few weeks later, my mom decided she was going to sell the house and she and my sisters were going to move in with a family friend. I didn't realize until a few weeks before the move that there would not be room for me at the friend's home. I was terrified. I was on my own again. I didn't know where I was going to live. I didn't know how I was going to support Asia. Rick came to me a few days later and asked me to marry him. I knew he was asking me because he wanted to help me. I reluctantly agreed. I was terrified, but I thought maybe he could save me from myself. He was such a kind and loving man and I will never understand how he could be so loving and stable while I was so mean, guarded, angry and unstable. I never even let myself become vulnerable and open emotionally to him until we were married for seven years.

Chapter 9

Rick and I were married in October. It was a small wedding at Rick's grandparents' home. His family helped with everything. His mother paid for almost everything. His aunt helped me pick the colors and designed all the decorations. They even prepared the food and arranged to have the photographs taken.

I was terrified to go through with the wedding but I told myself that his family had paid for everything and they would never forgive me if I didn't go through with it. In the end, I walked down the aisle and married my husband. It was a beautiful ceremony and I have never regretted having a small wedding. Asia was the flower girl. I couldn't bring myself to choose only one of my sisters as a maid of honor so I asked my best friend. There was so much turmoil going on in my family at that time, as a result of my parents' impending divorce.

My father chose not to come, because I was having someone else give me away. I was still very angry with him for the way he had abused me. I know this hurt him very deeply. I didn't realize that I could choose not to have someone give me away. I was trying to make everyone happy. I was resentful for years afterward that my father didn't come. I was also afraid to invite my foster family because I just didn't know how to handle it all without hurting someone's feelings. I look back now and wish that I had invited my foster family. I know they would've loved to have been there to support me. There was so much drama surrounding my wedding day, and I was afraid I wouldn't be able to make everyone happy.

A few weeks after we were married, I received a phone call at work from a woman who claimed that Asia was being sexually abused by her father. I was completely devastated. It was one of my worst nightmares come true. This was the thing that I was going to make sure never happened to my daughter.

Rick and I took her to the doctor that night to be examined. He said he couldn't be sure that she wasn't being abused. We called a lawyer and he said we couldn't keep Asia away from her father unless we could prove without a doubt that he was sexually abusing her. I thought God was punishing me again.

Over the next few weeks we sent Asia to counseling to see if there was any truth to the claims that this woman had made. Eventually the accusations were proven false. I was so relieved to find out that Asia was not suffering the abuse that I had as a child. Things finally calmed down in our lives.

At the time we were married we were both working full-time. By the next year we had bought a house and started down the road toward a mountain of debt. We didn't ask advice or listen to anyone. Rick's mother tried to tell us not to rush into things, but we decided that we knew more than anyone else.

I thought I couldn't stand it if we didn't get this house. All the inspections came back and we qualified as first time homebuyers, so we didn't need a down payment. We settled on our house in the winter right before Christmas of 1995. Our families helped us move in and we were able to get what we needed to furnish it from Rick's family. I thought because we had a house we would be happy. This couldn't have been further from the truth.

We were so far in debt, and had no budget. We just kept putting whatever we needed on credit cards; we believed that one day we would have the money we needed to pay everything off. I spent most of my time dreaming about how wonderful our life was going to be, instead of enjoying what we had.

Except for the debt we had created our life was very calm. I started to miss my drama, so I tried to create some wherever possible. I began to resent Rick for not being romantic or exciting enough, never being satisfied that this wonderful man loved me and my daughter and supported me in every way possible.

I went from job to job, but nothing would satisfy me. I would enjoy my job for a few months and then decide they were not paying me enough and they were taking advantage of me. I started working for a scrap metal plant, as a chief inventory clerk. I worked overtime to get the job done, but didn't get paid for the overtime. I thought that this made me valuable to them. I expected them to respect me for all the hard work I was doing. When I realized that they didn't appear to respect me, I got angry and walked out. I was able to get another job through a temporary agency about a week later.

I was hired as an executive assistant to the president and two vice presidents of an organization that supplied schools with educational equipment. Again, I started off like a power house. I did everything they asked of me and more. I went overboard in an attempt to make myself feel important. I imagined that they couldn't make it without me. Then I started to have health issues.

I continually contracted bronchitis and just struggled to get out of bed every morning. One day I woke up and my jaw was locked shut. I was only able to open it about a quarter of an inch. I couldn't eat any solid food. This went on for about three weeks. The pain was excruciating. I missed a lot of work and it was starting to affect my performance.

I went to the doctor and he sent me to a specialist. He took x-rays and told me that my jaw joint was badly damaged. He told me I needed a jaw replacement. The surgery cost $30,000 and we discovered that my insurance plan wouldn't cover it. Again, I blamed God for not giving me what I needed. I finally decided to take a medical leave of absence from my job.

My employers agreed to allow me medical leave and they even allowed me to collect disability. During the time I was on medical leave my doctor continued to pursue different avenues to obtain coverage for the surgery. He was unable to convince the insurance company to pay for the surgery.

This turned out to be a blessing in disguise. I started seeing a chiropractor who helped me regain the range of motion in my jaw. My situation was starting to improve and my medical leave was drawing to a close. I went back to my boss and told him I was ready to return to work. He informed me that if I wanted to come back it would be in another department and it would be a demotion. They had found a suitable replacement for me while I was gone. I couldn't believe they had found someone to replace me. Devastated, I decided to quit.

My daughter had seemed to enjoy having me home after school and I decided I would look for a job that would allow me to be home with her after school.

I continued to try to be the perfect mom to Asia. All the pressure made me constantly angry and no fun to be with. I became so overprotective and lived in fear that she would be taken from me. I was sure that God was going to punish me by taking away, what I believed, was the only good thing in my life.

After I quit my job, I was introduced to a network marketing company that promised that I had the ability to earn somewhere between $1,500 and $10,000 a month. This appealed to me, because I was looking for an easy way out. I was introduced to people who were said they were making $1,500 to $4,500 a month working part-time. This seemed like a dream come true. I thought that I would finally be able to make the money we needed to pay off our debt and have the life I'd always wanted.

We put the starter kit on a credit card and I set out to set the world on fire. We went to seminars and started talking to everyone we knew, asking them to join us. We signed up a few of our friends and started to sell some of the nutritional products.

I ended up using more product than I sold. I didn't have the skills or commitment to do what needed to be done to be successful. We continued to go further and further into debt. I kept charging more and more to our credit cards, hoping that things would turn around. I finally realized I needed to get a job to help support us until we could make this business work. Rick had really not been involved in the business with me but he didn't want to stand in the way of my dreams.

I was able to get a job as an assistant to a realtor. I worked part-time and was able to drive Asia to school in the morning and pick her up after school. We would have tea and a snack after school. I was trying to prove that I could work and be the world's best mom and wife. I worked with the realtor for a few years.

After working for the realtor a short time, I decided that the network marketing business was not for me. I ended my connection with them and decided to focus on real estate. My boss helped me get my real estate license and I worked hard to support her by taking care of her paperwork, showing houses and hosting open houses. I loved being in the real estate business but soon realized I couldn't be there for my family like I wanted to. I was still having health issues and missing work much more than I should have.

Asia woke up sick one morning and I called in sick. My boss and I both realized that this wasn't going to work for us anymore. I realized that being home for my daughter when she needed me was more important than a career. I had been working part-time as a nanny for a family with two boys as well as my job with the realtor. When the family I was working for, heard that I had quit my other job they asked me to come work full-time for them.

I thought I had found the thing I was meant to do with my life. I loved the two boys and I was able to take Asia to work with me. I started working full-time for them. They wanted me to clean the house, do the grocery shopping, make sure the boys did their homework, make dinner, etc. I settled in and really started enjoying my job. The boys stole my heart. I soon realized that their mom didn't really like doing things with them.

I planned field trips with them over the summer. We went to Baltimore Harbor, to parks for picnics, rented movies and played games together. Their mother started to resent my relationship with them. She started to require me to stay over every other Friday night so that her and her boyfriend could go out drinking. She wanted me to stay until the boys' grandparents came to pick them up on Saturday morning. I finally decided that this wasn't going to work. I didn't want to leave the boys, but didn't like the way things were turning out.

I decided I would start my own cleaning business. I contacted a few people that I knew from working in real estate and told them what I was doing. Work started to come in immediately. It was so exciting owning my own business and being my own boss. It was the first time I felt somewhat in control of my life. I was able to set my own hours and days to work. I could be home when my daughter was off school. I could take her to school in the morning and pick her up after school. It was a dream come true.

During the summer I had Asia help me. I paid her only five dollars a house. I thought she would be happy to have a little extra money for herself. After a couple of months I discovered that she had stolen a substantial amount of jewelry from one of my clients while we were cleaning. Luckily, the client was very gracious and didn't press charges. If she had decided to press charges it would have sent Asia into the juvenile system.

I started taking Asia to counseling and the counselor suggested she should make amends for the damage she had done.

Asia's father was not very supportive of the way I was handling this situation, but I knew that I had to make sure she knew that there were consequences to her actions. I really struggled with this situation, because I felt like I had failed her somehow. It seemed she was so angry with me and that she had done this to get back at me. Asia told me years later that it had a tremendous impact on her life, and I am sure that it kept her from making some other bad choices in her life.

I worked alone for the next few years. This worked out well; I could work at my own pace and listened to music while I cleaned. It relaxed me and I felt empowered. I built things up slowly over the years and eventually was given the opportunity to clean at a bed and breakfast part-time.

Working for the bed and breakfast didn't work very well. They wanted me to rush through the rooms and being a perfectionist, I just wasn't able to cope with rushing. I worked there a couple of months and when I started to get more private clients, I gave my notice.

Kate, the woman who had trained me when I started there informed me that she was looking for another job. I asked her to come into business with me. She agreed and we became business partners.

I was a little nervous at first, but it was nice after working alone all that time to have company and help while I worked. We became fast friends. We set out to create more work so that we could generate enough income for the both of us. Within a few months we had a very full schedule and were even having to turn down people from time to time because our schedule was so full.

One day I got a call from Sallie, Asia's father ex-fiancé. She told me that even though she was not dating Asia's father anymore, she wanted to continue to be part of Asia's life. I told her that I would like to meet with her because I wanted to get to know her a little bit before I allowed her to spend time with Asia. She heartily agreed, and we became very good friends. She was such a fun-loving, giving person. I could tell that Asia meant a lot to her and decided that she would make a good role model for Asia. She was like a second mom to Asia and we discovered that we had a lot in common.

God being the amazing Father He is began to soften my heart and I began going to church again. I tried attending a few and finally found one that seemed different. It was a non-denominational church and people wore jeans to church. This seemed like a place where they focused on God and not on appearances. I felt the presence of the Holy Spirit there. I thought I had found the place where I belonged.

I started to connect with God and bullied my family into going to church with me. Some good things came out of it but it was limited because I was more worried about changing my family, than working on myself.

My marriage was really struggling at this time and I wasn't sure our marriage would survive. The church sent us to a weekend marriage seminar and this was a turning point in our marriage. We came out of the weekend with a new vision for our marriage. We started to connect deeply for the first time since we had been married.

A few weeks later I learned that one of my cousins had killed himself. He was the kind of person who always seemed like he had it all together. I couldn't believe that he could do something like this. This sent me into a downward emotional spiral. I finally realized that this could've been me. I had been plagued by thoughts of suicide almost all my life and had begun to think that it was a normal part of everybody's life.

Chapter 10

My cousin's death shook me to my very core. I started to seek answers to the questions that were forming in my mind. I started Christian counseling in hopes of finding some answers. I wanted to know what caused these suicidal thoughts and what I could do to combat them. I started to look into our family history. I uncovered the long-hidden secret of mental illness in the family.

I discovered that out of the ten children my grandparents had, seven of them had tried to commit suicide. None of them had succeeded but I couldn't understand how this could've been hidden all these years. I started to realize that it was not normal to constantly think about killing myself.

God used my cousin's death to keep me alive for the next six years. Whenever I would descend into that deep dark place and think that everyone would be better off without me, I would remember what he had done. I realized how much it hurt all of those he had left behind. I always called my aunt, his mom, and talked to her whenever I felt this way. I never told her why I was calling, but it was enough to keep me from making the same horrible choice he had.

I continued my search for answers and a way to keep me from going down the same path that many others had chosen. One of my cousins gave me a book about bi-polar disorder. As I read, I was horrified to discover that out of the list of one hundred symptoms of the disorder, I exhibited nearly every single one. I remember showing the list of symptoms to Rick; he looked at the list and a look of shock came over his face. I realized that it was real. I did have these symptoms.

On one hand I was horrified and on the other I was relieved to discover that there was a reason for a lot of the internal struggles I had suffered all of my life. Terrified, I continued my research and finally made an appointment with a doctor to discuss my diagnosis. He prescribed some medication to help even out my moods. It seemed to work very well. It slowed down the racing thoughts I had always been plagued with.

I continued with my counseling and started to deal with the abuse from my childhood again. I hoped that this time I could finally get past all the anger and rage I felt and find true healing. After a while the medication began to make me feel numb. I felt like I couldn't feel excited anymore. I started bruising all over my body. I called the doctor and he said I had to have some blood work done. I decided to discontinue the medication.

It was right after this that my sister, Toni, announced her plans to get married. I was excited for her and couldn't wait to help her celebrate. I was just starting to deal with my childhood abuse and the prospect of spending so much time with my mother and father made me nervous. I didn't think I was strong enough.

I wasn't able to sleep for days before the wedding and the day of the wedding I was exhausted. When Rick and I arrived at the church, it was apparent that they didn't need my help. Once again, I felt like the outsider. I was so wounded, but I tried to keep it to myself. It didn't work out very well.

When we got to the reception I realized that they had seated me beside my father. I couldn't believe it. I expressed my anger and my sister Terri overheard me. I realized too late that I was making a scene and that I needed to leave so I wouldn't ruin my sister's wedding. Unfortunately, Toni found out and she was angry. As a result, we did not speak to each other again for several years. I tried to find a way to make amends, but it was too late. The damage was done and it seemed that nothing could fix it.

My counselor told me that I needed to stop dwelling on the loss and move on. I didn't know how to do this. As a result, I missed my sister, Terri's wedding the following year. I didn't trust myself. I didn't want to do the wrong thing. I didn't want to go through the pain of loss again, so I chose to stay away. I missed a lot as a result.

I missed being there to see my sister get married to the man she had loved for many years. This time I chose to be the outsider. I think I thought if I made the choice to be excluded it would hurt less. I was wrong.

I missed seeing my nephew and niece being born. I found out my sister was pregnant from a neighbor. The pain of knowing she didn't want me in her life was so severe; I thought I would not survive. Again, I focused on what I had lost. It would be years before I would stop blaming others for this loss and realize the part I had played in creating the situation.

I had been seeing a chiropractor and he introduced me to some natural methods of managing the bi-polar disorder. I started to change my diet, got rid of refined sugar in my diet, and started trying to get regular exercise. I started to notice that Asia was exhibiting symptoms of bi-polar disorder as well. So I started to change her diet as well. I went to extremes to radically reduce her sugar intake. I wanted to make sure that she didn't go through years in the dark as I had.

I made so many drastic changes in our lives that it was impossible to maintain. We continued to attend church for a few years. I had really felt like I was part of the church family. Slowly I started to realize that things were not as they seemed. I felt disconnected, but still continued to attend out of obligation. I met a couple through the church that had been going to a counselor that had been very effective in helping them. They gave me his business card and I contacted him to set up an appointment.

As soon as I met J.R. Fisher, I knew that this was unlike any counseling I had ever been through. First of all, he only charged me a minimal amount based on our income. When I walked into his office I was scared to death but there was something about his demeanor that set me at ease immediately. He informed me that the Holy Spirit would be guiding our session and that if I was willing to go deep I would experience true healing. We began with prayer and then he asked me what I was seeing. One clear memory God brought to my mind was the time when, as a little girl in Florida, my mom had locked me out of the house.

Jesus came into that memory with me and brought an end to the lie that Satan had told to me at that moment. He told me that I was not loved, and not special. Jesus told me that He loved and cherished me. I began to experience healing from emotional pain I had suffered with for over thirty years. I began to realize that I had believed Satan's lies all my life and that was the source of my torment, not God.

I continued to meet with J.R. for a few months and decided that Asia should come with me. J.R. told me that she should come into the sessions with me so that she would be able to experience healing as well. We went to counseling for a while and I did experience some breakthrough and healing. Through theophostic healing I was able to let go of my resentment against my father and my mother. At this point I thought God was finished and I was completely healed and whole. I did feel so much better than I had in years. The healing I received did go a long way in improving my relationship with my husband and daughter.

During this time the cleaning business was picking up and Kate and I decided to break up into two teams and hire a few people to help us. We went out in two separate areas. I met a woman at my church, named Bethany, who had recently had a baby and needed work. I asked her if she would be willing to work for me. She agreed and brought her baby along and worked alongside me.

We hit it off immediately. We both were perfectionists and preferred working at a slower pace. I found out she was born and raised in Florida and was planning on moving back. We worked together for about six months. We would talk about God, our past, and our shared love of Florida.

She really encouraged me that I would one day be able to move to Florida. It had been my lifelong dream since my family had left when I was young. I told everyone I knew that someday I was going to move back to Florida. There was always a part of me that didn't believe I was worthy to see this dream realized but then there was a part of me that refused to let the dream die. Bethany moved to Florida after a few months and I thought I might never see her again. God had different plans!

Chapter 11

The church we were going to seemed to be faltering and my husband and daughter just stopped wanting to go. I was so angry and couldn't understand why God wasn't changing my family. I started to have panic attacks and health issues, and started missing church. A short time later I started to feel disconnected from the church. I stopped feeling like the pastor's message was touching me. I missed a few weeks of church and realized that my mailbox had been removed. I felt rejected and alone again. I finally decided that church was not for me.

Throughout the time I was seeking God, He began to work through circumstances in my life. My health was deteriorating and my relationship with Asia was still struggling no matter how many counseling sessions we went to.

Asia's father approached me on Mother's Day of 2005 and announced that he had decided he wanted custody of Asia. This was devastating to me when I realized that she had decided she wanted to live with him. Rick and I contacted a lawyer to discuss our rights. At the same time I took Asia to a Christian counselor to try to handle this situation without resentment and anger. During the time we were fighting for custody of Asia I fell into deep despair. I thought losing Asia was inevitable and another punishment from God for not being righteous enough.

I asked advice of nearly everyone I knew. Almost everyone I sought advice from told me that since Asia was fourteen she could choose where she wanted to live and there was nothing I would be able to do about it. Others told me that if I did manage to keep custody of Asia she would resent me for it and I would lose her anyway. The Christian counselor we were working with also told me that I needed to allow Asia to make this choice on her own.

I wanted to give up, but just couldn't bring myself to give up my daughter without a fight. Again, as in my childhood, I felt like it was me against the world. Finally, a friend of mine told me that I needed to listen to that nagging feeling that I had. She encouraged me to fight for custody of Asia. I was still unsure of what to do, and was not feeling supported in my view that I knew what was best for my daughter.

Asia's father and I met with the counselor prior to a scheduled mediation, that was created to help us come to a mutual agreement about what was in the best interests of Asia. I reluctantly agreed to allow her father to have primary custody of her. That night when I went home our lawyer called, and I informed him of the decision we had reached. He told me that despite what I had been told, it was not a fact that Asia could choose where she wanted to live. He said that the judge would decide what was in Asia's best interest not necessarily what she wanted. At that moment I decided I would fight for Asia. Throughout this process I was in complete emotional turmoil.

I finally cried out to God and said that I wanted Him to control the situation. I told Him that I would trust Him to do what was best for Asia. At this moment a tremendous peace washed over me that I could not explain. I realized that this was the peace that passes all understanding that I had heard about all my life. This was the first time that I had ever experienced this peace. I went to bed and slept better than I had since this situation had begun.

When we went before the mediator the next day I was still a little nervous but I knew it was going to work out for our best. The mediator started off asking Asia's father why he was fighting for primary custody of her. Asia was doing well in school and seemed to be well adjusted. He said that he loved his daughter and wanted to spend more time with her. Then an amazing thing happened. The mediator asked me if I would agree to allow Asia's father to have dinner with her one extra night each week. This would not officially change our custody arrangement but still give her father more time with her.

I was reminded of Solomon and the wisdom he displayed when the two women had come before him asking for his judgment in their situation. Both of these women were mothers. One child was dead and the other was alive. Both of the women insisted that the child that was alive was hers. King Solomon in his wisdom said, "Let's take a sword and divide the living child in half and give each woman half of the child." One of the women pleaded with him and asked him not to harm the child. She said that the other woman was the baby's mother so that the child's life would be spared. The other woman said let not the child be mine or yours, but divide him. King Solomon knew instantly that the woman who wished to spare the child's life was indeed the real mother. That evening my lawyer called and informed me that Asia's father had decided to drop the custody suit. Everything went back to normal. God had brought me through my circumstances again. This was the first time I had a glimpse of the true nature of God. This lead me to begin to have faith in God's will for my life.

Things were very rocky for a few years, but eventually my relationship with Asia's father improved. By the grace of God, I was able to lay aside the anger and resentment I had so long held against him. His mother passed away and he asked me to attend the funeral. It was another opportunity for healing. I was able to see all of Tina's children and tell them how sorry I was that I hadn't been able to stay and take care of them. They really reached out to me. It was so heartwarming. Asia's father also told me how much he admired me for being such a great mom. I had struggled for years with guilt over not being the mother Asia needed and those words touched my heart deeply. All the years of anger and blame just melted away. We were able to start to have a team approach to raising Asia after that.

Chapter 12

In 2008 Rick and I decided to give up the financial fight. We were drowning in debt and could see no light at the end of the tunnel. We tried debt counseling, but were unable to pay even the minimal payment that was needed to maintain the payoff of the debt we had created. After struggling for a few months we finally made the difficult decision to file for bankruptcy. I was mortified. I thought that I would never be able to rise above the guilt I felt. Our lawyer told us we could file Chapter Seven and still be able to keep our house and cars. The law firm we were using was in Tennessee and we got lost in the shuffle of the masses that were filing bankruptcy.

The process was dragged out for several months. During this long drawn out process Rick started to hear rumors that there was going to be layoffs at the company he worked for. I couldn't believe it. I thought it was some kind of punishment for proceeding with the bankruptcy. I knew we wouldn't be able to pay the mortgage on the house without his job. My health had affected my ability to work a full-time job and I didn't know what we were going to do. I called Kate and cried on her shoulder. I told her that my lifelong dream of moving to Florida was slipping right through my fingers. I will never forget her next words. She said, "Tammy you can be just as broke in Florida as you are here." She went on to say that we could surrender our house and take what we could and move to Florida to start over. I realized she was right. I started to wish for Rick to be laid off.

During this time God called me back to work with J.R. again. This time I went deep and was set free from the suicidal thoughts forever. I remember at our last session the last vision I saw was Jesus and me driving down the road in a red convertible. It gave me such peace and I knew that God was getting ready to do some great things in my life. I thought everything was going to be downhill from there. Boy was I wrong. The battle had only begun.

God reminded me of Bethany. I still had her cell phone number, so I called her up and explained to her what was going on. She said that there were plenty of jobs in the area they lived in for people in the air conditioning installation business. So I created a new resume for Rick and got online to search for jobs. I found several ads for jobs in Stuart, Florida and the surrounding areas. The next month he was laid off and I sprang into action.

I contacted our mortgage company and told them that we were filing bankruptcy; my husband had no job and I didn't know what to do. I found out that due to the high incidence of foreclosed homes in the area that it could take the bank as long as a year to come to take the property. I couldn't stand the thought that the bank could come lock the doors while we were away and we would have nowhere to go. Then I remembered Sallie, Asia's second mom, and got the crazy idea to ask her if we could live with her until we could afford to move to Florida.

I called her and explained the situation and asked her if we could move into her basement bedroom. To my complete surprise she agreed. She not only agreed to allow us to live with her but also agreed that we could bring our cats with us as well. I was blessed beyond words. The only problem was we would have to move out of Asia's school district. Sallie's home was about a forty-five minute drive from where we lived. We wouldn't be able to drive her to school each morning.

Rick and I discussed it and decided to talk to Asia and her father to see if she could move in with him for the last five months of school. He and Asia agreed and we started putting things in motion. I checked into the cost of moving the furniture to Florida and realized that it was more expensive to move the furniture than the value of the actual furniture. It was a no brainer for me to get rid of our furniture and start over.

We placed ads in Craigslist and sold and gave away almost everything we owned. It was so weird selling things day by day. We had some very supportive friends who bought a large portion of our belongings to help us reach our goal. We sold our water bed and started to sleep on an air mattress. Little by little everything started to sell. Every time something else sold I was excited to see that we were that much closer to reaching our dream. We sat on camp chairs in the living room after the sofa, chair and loveseat were gone. Then someone came by and bought our oven, so we started to have to eat takeout. The house was empty and I couldn't wait to move out.

I continued packing our personal belongings over the few weeks that we were selling our furniture. Finally the day came when Asia moved to her father's house. I couldn't believe how hard it was for me. I knew she was graduating in a couple of months and going to be going into the Navy but I was not ready for her to leave yet. I cried for hours after she left.

A few days later we moved into Sallie's home. I really enjoyed living with Sallie; she went out of her way to make us feel at home. If she would have lived in Florida, I probably would still be living with her. She had two beautiful huskies that would wake Rick and me up around six every morning with their singing. God had blessed us in so many ways.

I started to mail and email Rick's resume out to companies all over the West Palm Beach and Martin County area. We scheduled a vacation and planned to stay with Bethany and her husband for a few weeks so Rick could go on job interviews and drop off more resumes. We packed up what we could fit in both our cars and headed south.

We arrived at Bethany and Chad's home and the next day Rick and I traveled around Martin County dropping off resumes and he was able to go on a few job interviews. He was offered a job and they wanted him to start immediately. We were ecstatic; he would be starting out making more money than he ever had made before. He decided to take it and we set out to find an apartment. We found an apartment to rent and moved the things we had in storage into our new apartment. I was afraid I was going to wake up and find out it was all a dream. It seemed too good to be true. We couldn't believe our good fortune.

While we were visiting, we began attending the church our friends attended and I knew that we belonged. The pastor was so down to earth. His messages were so powerful; they were full of God's grace and mercy. He talked plainly from his heart and it was clear that God was speaking through this man. He talked about the transformation God had performed in his life and it gave me hope for the future.

We had moved into the apartment and I was anxious to go back to Pennsylvania to be with Asia for her senior prom and graduation. I left to return on my own and Rick remained in Florida to work. It was difficult to leave Rick but I knew we were working toward a bright future together. We were living the dream. Asia was leaving in July to enter the nuclear program in the Navy, so I felt free to move.

Rick started attending the church while he was on his own. Every week when we talked he would inform me that he had been attending church. I couldn't believe it. He was attending without me doing anything. I continued to thank God for this but part of me kept wondering if this would continue.

Rick flew back to Pennsylvania in time for Asia's graduation and her graduation party. The next day we packed up my car, including our three cats, and set off towards Florida. I dropped Rick off at the Airport so he could get back home to work and then continued on my way. It seemed like a dream. I couldn't believe that God had opened the path for us to move so easily. I had my plan all mapped out. Life was going to be good.

I was able to visit with a friend in North Carolina on the way down. It wasn't much of a visit because my cats were freaking out. They screamed the entire journey. They must have been completely horrified; they had already been through so much. When I finally reached Stuart, Florida, I remember thinking, "I made it!" I was so happy to finally have made my dream come true. My dream was soon to become a nightmare.

About two weeks after I had arrived in Florida, Asia came down to visit us. She was supposed to be leaving for basic training in July. She had injured her knee back in May and we were hoping she would heal so that she was able to make it through the Navy's basic training. While she was with us, we realized that her knee would need more time to heal and the Navy recruiter said that she would have to be discharged and re-enlist when her knee was healed. That same day Rick was laid off from his job. At first, I thought he would quickly be able to find another job. I thought we would be okay and God would provide.

Rick began sending his resume out looking for work and no one would call him back. I couldn't understand what was happening. What about the vision I had of Jesus and me in the red convertible. God was not blessing our plans! I felt like God had just pulled the rug out from under me.

Asia went back home to be with her father for a little while. She struggled over the end of her dream of going into the Navy. She called me a few weeks later and asked if she could come live in Florida with Rick and me. I couldn't believe it! One of the reasons I had waited so long to move to Florida was that she had said she never wanted to live there. I agreed and couldn't wait for her to come.

Her father gave her money to fly down and since Rick and I had an apartment with two bedrooms and two full bathrooms, we had plenty of room. She started to attend church with us. She tried to keep herself from being close to anyone, because after all this was just a stop over until she could re-enlist into the Navy.

We continued to attend the church and for the first time I started to learn about the grace and mercy of God. I learned even though I wasn't worthy, but that Jesus had made me worthy. I held onto Jeremiah 29:11 during this time. "For I know the plans I have for you", declares the Lord, "plans to prosper you and not to harm you, plans to give you a hope and a future." I kept saying that over and over again, at the same time getting angrier the longer it took God to open the door. I didn't know what God was waiting for. I fell into deep despair. I started to believe that I had hoped for too much. I thought I just needed to settle down and start surviving life. I needed to focus on heaven and how wonderful it was going to be then.

During this time we grew connected with our church and became part of the family. These people really reached out to us. Rick and I came home one afternoon and found a bag of groceries on our porch. I was so touched that someone would go out of their way to bring us food. We began attending a small group and developing friendships. My lack of self-worth and the deep disappointment that I felt toward God continued to make it difficult for me to connect very deeply with anyone.

Chapter 13

Rick was able to get a job and I was hired as a part-time receptionist in October of 2009. I thought now things are going to turn around. Asia was able to get a job as well. However, Rick's job only lasted a month and he was laid off again. They told him he would be hired back as soon as work picked back up, but we waited in vain for several months.

No matter how hard things were, I still woke up every morning thankful to be living in Florida. I could go to the beach anytime I wanted and the weather was much easier on my body. After suffering through the cold winters up North it was a welcome change. Still I continued to hope for God to change our circumstances.

One evening during the time we were struggling, I logged onto Facebook one evening and couldn't believe my eyes when I saw my foster mom's name there. I messaged her and hoped she would be happy to hear from me after the years of separation. She messaged me back and I sent her my phone number and we spoke for about an hour. She told me how happy she was to hear my voice again. She was so thrilled to hear me call her mom. I told her she would always be my mom. It was enormously healing. I couldn't believe after all these years that my foster family still wanted me to be in their lives.

In August of 2010, Asia had to go back to Pennsylvania to be in her cousin's wedding. We started to look for a deal on airfare, but prices were pretty high. I finally asked her if I could drive her. I thought it would be nice to be able to visit everyone at home and let them know I was doing well. I called Mom to let her know I was coming for a visit and wanted to take some time to visit with the family. Asia and I called Sallie and made arrangements to stay with her during our visit.

During our visit Asia and I were able to have lunch with Mom, Kristi and her son, Colton, Kerry and his daughter Trinity. It was like all the years of separation melted away the moment we saw each other. We had a wonderful time together, but it was far too short. We made arrangements to meet at Kristi's and Barry's house the day before Asia and I were scheduled to leave. We were there for a little while and I was happy to see everyone, but longed to see Gail.

When she walked in the door I was blown away. We looked at each other and then ran toward each other and held onto each other crying for several minutes. I hadn't realized how much I missed her until she was standing in front of me. We laughed together and talked for hours. As we talked I realized that she had been telling her children all about me over the years we had been apart. I realized that she was the sister that I always wanted. I had spent so many years trying to have the relationship with my sisters that I already had with Gail.

Asia and I had such a hard time leaving because we enjoyed being with my family so much. Asia and I headed home the next day and we were anxious to get back home, but we left a piece of our hearts in Pennsylvania with my family. It had been an amazing journey of healing for both Asia and me.

While we were gone, Rick had been able to start working part-time for a small air-conditioning installation company. Things seemed to be going well, but after we came home the work started to slow down. Again, I started to wonder what God was doing.

Rick and I were really struggling under the financial pressure and I was afraid our marriage wouldn't survive. We started to meet with our pastor once a week. That first meeting, Rick gave his life to Christ. I was so excited, and thought that now everything would fall into place. Life was going to be wonderful! Our pastor told us to start praying together every night before bed. Rick agreed and we started praying together. Things didn't seem to change much and I started to settle into my doubts and unbelief again.

Shortly after Asia and I returned from Pennsylvania, my boss offered me full-time work and I decided to take it. Rick's unemployment had run out and I thought it was up to me to save the day again. I couldn't understand what was taking God so long. Rick was able to get a part-time job shortly after I started working full-time. The job was taking a toll on me and I was becoming resentful. It seemed no matter how hard we tried we couldn't make enough money to pay for even our basic needs.

While we were struggling to survive I kept pleading with God to show me what I needed to do to receive His blessing on our lives. It was during this time that my pastor taught out of a passage in Mark one Sunday in 2010, and these two verses clicked in my spirit. This portion of scripture has become especially close to my heart – It's Mark 9:23-24 Jesus was talking to a man whose son was possessed by a demon, and the disciples had tried to cast the demon out and failed. So the father came to Jesus and asked him to help them if he could. The man's reply resonated with me and I began to pray, "God, I believe, but help my unbelief!" I cried out to God this way for months, pleading with Him to help me believe.

Shortly after this God lead me to start joining the prayer before our Sunday church services. I was so self-conscious about praying out loud in front of other people. Over time it started to become comforting for me to pray with the group of prayer warriors in our church. I started to be calmer and more peaceful. I also started to notice small changes in Rick and Asia.

After a few months, one of my friends from our church small group asked us to come support her when she shared her testimony at Celebrate Recovery. I remember thinking, "Wow, what a nice program for 'other' people who need healing, but this isn't for me."

God began transforming my life and the life of my family radically over the next year. By the end of 2010 my husband had given his life to Christ and finally had gotten a full-time job, I was led to Celebrate Recovery and Asia was led to go to YWAM (Discipleship Training School).

Next thing I knew, God was leading me to go to the Friday night meetings at Celebrate Recovery. I attended, never really feeling connected, but I couldn't keep myself from going. Even Rick told me I should go, and said that he noticed I always felt better when I went.

Chapter 14

I came to Celebrate Recovery crippled by fear and worry. I wanted so desperately to believe that God had my best interests at heart. I was angry and felt defeated most of the time. My marriage was still struggling and I was afraid it might fall apart. I kept asking God to show me the answers, and felt like He wasn't even listening.

During the year and a half that Rick had been looking for work, I was able to sharpen my resumé writing skills. I was able to help some other people with their resumes. My small group leader asked me how much I would charge to write someone's resumé so he could pass the word along. I started to think maybe I could make a business out of this. I worked on a few people's resumés and told them to pay me what they felt it was worth. I was paid a substantial amount by two of them, and decided that this was a sign from God. I decided to start a resumé writing business on the side.

I ordered some business cards and began to put the word out that I was beginning a resumé writing business. Things were moving very slowly. I really wanted to be able to quit my job and I decided that maybe I should start a cleaning business at the same time. I still didn't believe that

I deserved to be successful at anything other than cleaning. I decided since I had already had some success at cleaning that I should stick with what I knew and stop dreaming that I deserved to do anything different.

I put an ad on Craigslist and started with a few clients. I soon felt led to leave my part-time job and pursue my cleaning business full-time. Asia decided she would quit her job and help me with the cleaning business. After all, she was going to be leaving in June to go to YWAM. I had hatched the brilliant idea that I could build up a cleaning business and hire someone to run it while I continued to work at my resumé writing business. I soon decided to start up a pet sitting business on the side as well. All the while, I was fighting my feelings of inadequacy and unworthiness. I thought that I didn't really deserve to succeed at the resumé business.

In January of 2011, Rick was able to find a full-time job and God told me He wanted me to join the Step Study at Celebrate Recovery. God and I struggled over this. I had several excuses for why I shouldn't be a part of the Step Study. It wasn't my kind of thing. God had already healed me from so much pain, and the rest of the work was up to me, etc. God finally asked me if I was willing to do what I needed to do to make lasting change in my life. This convinced me to step out in faith and obey God's leading.

When I first came into the class, I couldn't understand why God had called me to be part of this study. I didn't feel like I had anything in common with any of these women. As the weeks went by, I started to become connected with the other women in the group. I couldn't wait each week for class. One of the requirements was that we had to make three connections with our sisters in our group each week. I didn't like this, but I wanted to follow the rules. I started to feel connected and safe with these women. I was still not ready to completely lower my mask, but I couldn't stay away from the weekly meetings.

My husband and I continued to struggle with our finances. The year and a half that my husband had been unemployed had taken a tremendous toll on our financial situation. I was so angry. I felt like God was not keeping His promise to provide for all our needs. It seemed the harder we worked the farther behind we would get. My health really began to suffer again in the beginning of 2011. I was trying to burn the candle at both ends.

Asia had made the decision to go to YWAM at the end of 2010 and I shifted into high gear. We began to make jewelry in order to raise the money she needed for her tuition. I wanted to trust God to provide what she needed but I didn't know how. I thought we somehow had to earn

His favor. I felt like it was up to me to make sure that she could follow God's plan. I didn't even consider that God could and would bring in the money that she needed to do what He was calling her to do. He could do that without my help. Instead of trusting Him to provide the money for her, I continued to look for Him to start blessing us financially so we could support Asia.

Asia decided she wanted to go back to Pennsylvania for a visit before she left for her Discipleship Training School with YWAM. I started thinking I'd like to go with her. She said she would love to be able to drive back to Pennsylvania together again. I began to struggle with my desire to go back with Asia and my fear that we would not have the money to go. I felt very selfish thinking about taking a trip with Asia while we were struggling so hard financially.

One Sunday while we were at church, I was struggling with this decision. In the middle of the message I heard God say that He wanted me to go to Pennsylvania with Asia. He told me to trust Him that this was exactly the time on my Celebrate Recovery journey for me return to Pennsylvania. He said that He would provide what we needed and He wanted me to stop worrying. I didn't understand how this was going to happen but a tremendous peace washed over me and I knew that we were going to go to Pennsylvania. After that things began to fall into place for our trip. Even Rick was sure that we should go, so I let go of the guilt and fear and started to plan our trip.

The morning before we were supposed to leave, I woke up from a vivid dream. The dream was about the car and when I woke up I had an incredible urge to take the car into the garage and have it looked at again. I had taken the car into the shop earlier in the week, so I ignored this feeling. Asia and I set off for Pennsylvania the next day and I put the dream out of my mind.

On the journey we listened to music from my past. It brought back a lot of memories from my past. God started to remind me of people I had forgotten about a long time ago. I was able to bring up a lot of hurts that God wanted to heal but also some really wonderful memories as well. I couldn't wait to get to Pennsylvania to see all the people we hadn't been able to see for such a long time.

I regretted the decision not to have the car checked out again when we reached Virginia in the early morning hours, with the engine tapping. We didn't know where it would be safe to stop and have it checked out, so I prayed and asked God to help us reach our destination. We arrived in Pennsylvania and I took the car to a garage to have it checked out. It had only a half a quart of oil left in the engine. We had the oil changed and had the engine flushed. It seemed to be okay so we continued on.

When we arrived at my sister's house it felt good. Terri was clearly happy to have us visit. I didn't have any expectations on how I wanted her to treat me. We just enjoyed each other's company. There was healing for me during the weekend we stayed with her. For the first time in the history of my relationship with my sister I felt free to be myself with her. It was a wonderful feeling that I never dreamed I would be able experience.

Asia and I went to a cookout at Kristi and Barry's. I was able to spend some time with Kerry and see what God was doing in his life. I was in awe of how God had delivered him from addiction and turned him around. He has a heart for God and such a passion to reach the people who are still lost. It was so encouraging to hear what God had been doing in his life.

Little Denny also came to visit. I wasn't sure if he would remember me. He told me I was silly to think he would've forgotten me. Kerry and Little Denny took Asia and me for a ride on their motorcycles. It was amazing! They took us by the old farmhouse we used to live in when I was growing up. There were so many wonderful memories attached to this place.

Asia and I were having such a wonderful time we didn't want to leave. I was able to have some time with Gail. She had offered to let me stay with her for a few days. I could see she was struggling so desperately to keep her life together. We spent the first night I stayed over talking about all the old times and how much fun we had. We stayed up very late talking and that wonderful feeling from all those years ago came back. I found myself wishing that I could bring Gail home to Florida with me.

The next day when I went out to the car the engine light came on. Little Denny was a mechanic so I went out to pick him up from work so he could look at the car. He was able to identify what was wrong with it and he offered to fix it for me. We went out and bought the part he needed and he fixed the car for me the next day. He didn't want to take any money but I gave him a little bit anyway, wishing it could be more. It warmed my heart to see the wonderful man that he had grown into. He still has that grin that used to melt my heart and that was wonderful to see.

The day after Denny had fixed the car, Asia and I decided we needed to leave for home. I was able to stop in to see my sister, Toni before we left. We had a wonderful visit and we were able to make amends for some of the things that had happened in the past. After that visit I left to pick up Asia so we could begin the journey home.

For the first time in my life, I felt at peace with my past. I realized that Florida had truly become my home. I no longer thought of Pennsylvania as my home, even though I knew I would continue to miss many of my friends and loved ones. All in all it was an amazing journey. God brought much revelation and some healing during the journey.

I came home ready to continue my Step Study and really dig in with God. I was ready to do an extensive personal inventory with God and view my life's experiences through His eyes. I finally realized one of the reasons that God had brought me to Celebrate Recovery. Theophostic healing had taken the boulders out of my pathway toward Jesus and Celebrate Recovery was there to remove the pebbles that still remained. I realized that pebbles don't seem like much until they're in your shoe and make it difficult for you to walk the life God has asked you to walk. God made it clear that He wanted me to get rid of everything that was in the way of the plan He had for me.

Chapter 15

Through the Celebrate Recovery program God continued to reveal to me His true nature. I began to see that God had accepted me right where I was, but He was not content to leave me there. This God promised in Joel 2:25, that He would repay me for the years the locusts have eaten. I held onto that verse for dear life, because over the years I thought that most of my life was wasted. I didn't think that God would be able to use me because of the many bad choices I had made. This God promised He would walk through any trial with me. This God promised He would provide all I could ever need. This God shows me mercy, grace, and unconditional love. God didn't change; just my perception of who He is has changed.

Through my Celebrate Recovery Step Study all the things I had heard for years about God became rooted in my heart, where the enemy couldn't steal them from me. I realized God's mighty power. I realized that when "God decided to do something there was no one on earth and no devil in hell that could stop Him," another saying I've taken from Joyce Meyer. My constant worry over our financial struggles diminished greatly after going through the program. I started to crave the abundant life that Jesus had died to give me.

After returning from the trip back to Pennsylvania, my faith in God was strengthened and I was refreshed, energized and ready to take on the world. Asia, however, was getting ready to go to YWAM and she started to really shut down. I was so excited for her to take this journey with God and couldn't understand why she seemed so angry all the time. She didn't seem to want to do anything to prepare herself for her trip. I was trying to step back and allow her to make her own choices, but all I could see was that she was messing up her life.

The day before she was supposed to leave she decided to stay out very late with her friends. It broke my heart to think that she didn't want to spend the evening with me. It seemed as though she was trying to hurt me in any way possible. We ended up saying horrible things to each other that night. I couldn't sleep because I was so angry with myself for choosing to try and control her on her last night here. I wrote her a note apologizing for my behavior and slipped it into her suitcase. We got up very early to take her to the airport, and it seemed she couldn't get away fast enough. I hoped that when she arrived in Texas that she would find the card and call to apologize. That didn't happen. What I didn't realize at the time was that she had decided she didn't want to go to YWAM the week before she left. The enemy was working hard to keep her from the plan God had for her life. She was angry at God, the world and me because I was so cheerful and excited for her. She wanted to run away from everyone and everything, and especially God.

She finally called me late that day and the conversation we had was heartbreaking for me. She seemed so angry at me and I felt so hurt. I realized that she was gone and I felt so alone. God started to show me how dependent I had become on her. There was no room for me to have a relationship with my husband, because I was too busy trying to have the perfect relationship with my daughter. He showed me that I was trying to live vicariously through her. I had given up on doing anything with my life, because I had lost hope that God could use me. The first week she was gone, I couldn't pass her empty room without crying.

At the same time I was grieving Asia being gone, I found out that one of my cousins had been in a horrible accident. He was young, and had a young daughter. He was my aunt and uncle's only child. He was in critical condition for a week or two. We were all praying that he would pull through and that God would heal him. It became apparent that his brain had sustained too much damage and his parents had to make the painful decision to turn off the machines that were keeping his body functioning.

God convicted me of how selfish and self-centered I had been. My daughter was alive and she was walking in God's will for her life. I had so much to be thankful for, but once again I was having a big pity party for myself. I was able to speak with Asia that day. God had begun to soften her heart and she was so excited about what He was showing her. I realized that I needed God's help so I could let her go. I knew if I didn't let her go it would slow down the process God was taking her through. I decided to become a partner with God and allow Him to start guiding me. No more pity party for me. God told me we had a lot of work to do and very little time. I surrendered my plans and dreams to God once again and began looking forward to what He had in store for me.

My cousin's death had a strong impact on my family. The cousins set up a family Facebook account, so that we could stay connected. One of my cousins revealed that our grandfather had started to write a book about his life. He had gone through my grandfather's papers after his death and discovered what he had started to write. My cousin typed out what he could decipher and published it on Facebook.

When I read it I was blown away by the relationship my grandfather had with God. His story revealed how he became saved and then he went on to talk about how God had led him through many things in his life. I realized that the strongholds in our family had started to be broken with him and his trust in God. There were so many things that he had experienced that I had never known about. When I read that story, I remember feeling so cheated that he had never finished his book. He had so many wonderful stories to tell about how God had impacted his life and now there was no one left to tell them.

During the rest of the year, I spent a lot of time seeking God's plan for my life. I continually prayed and asked Him what He wanted me to do for His kingdom. I talked a lot to Him, but didn't take much time to listen. I started diving into the Bible and attending any extra teaching I could find. Throughout this process I started to get the message from Him that He loved me. I thought, "I know you love me, God." He kept repeating the message of His love for me through many different people.

During a prayer soaking I was attending I saw a vision of many of the women in the Bible that Jesus had met: the Samaritan woman at the well, the Canaanite woman who had pleaded for her son's healing, the prostitute, the woman who was healed when she touched the hem of Jesus' garment. After each woman, I saw Jesus face. He was smiling at me. I could clearly see the love on His face. I didn't understand what this meant. I shared it with everyone in the room, and another woman who was there said that Jesus told her to tell me how much He loved me. She went on to say that I needed to know I had God's approval and to stop seeking the approval of man. I was starting to get really impatient. I thought, "Yea, yea, yea, I know you love me, now what do you what me to do?"

The message He was trying to give me didn't sink in until I was listening to a teaching by Joyce Meyer one morning. She was talking about John, the disciple whom Jesus loved. She said that Peter was always going around talking about how much He loved Jesus, but John was always calling himself the disciple whom Jesus loved. She went on to say that John was the disciple that survived the longest. They had tried to boil him in oil and couldn't kill him. God spoke to me in my spirit saying, "You are the disciple whom I love!" I started saying that out loud to myself several times a day. The message that Jesus had been trying to get through to me finally began to take hold of me. God wanted me to receive His love. Until I fully received His love, I wouldn't be able to really show love to others. I can't give away what I don't have. This was a major breakthrough for me. It was the beginning of learning how to walk in the peace that God says I have.

Chapter 16

In September, my sister Toni, and her husband came to Florida for a vacation. She called me to schedule time to come to see Rick and me. I couldn't believe that she wanted to take time out of her vacation to visit with me. We went to the beach for a little, and it was wonderful to see the children playing in the water. Their visit was far too short, but I was able to make amends again for my part in our separation. We also started talking about getting together for a vacation together in the next few years. I enjoyed seeing the children and was deeply touched that they enjoyed spending time with me.

I started to really dig in with God and became so dependent on Him that I couldn't start the day without spending time with Him. Slowly I started to notice changes in my attitude. During this time Asia was in Peru on her outreach with YWAM. We did not have the ability to talk with her during this time because her cell phone did not work outside of the country.

One night I was awakened with an overwhelming feeling of dread. I just kept feeling like I had to pray for Asia. A thought came into my head that she was going to die in Peru. I started to pray fervently and said out loud that she was with God and He was going to protect her. I couldn't stop praying for her for three days and then that feeling of dread went away.

Asia called me a few weeks later, to let me know that she had just returned to the U.S. She shared a little bit about her trip with me. She told me that she had been very sick for three days. The doctor had to give her breathing treatments when they were in the mountains. We both realized that it was the exact time that I had the overwhelming desire to pray for her. I was amazed that God would stir me to pray for her when she needed it most. It gave me the revelation that I know longer needed to worry, because God was in control. I had heard that all my life but that experience gave me a deeper knowledge of what it meant for God to be in control.

That same morning the realtor for our landlord called me and said that the landlord was planning to evict us. This shocked me, because we had been working very hard to catch up on the rent. We had been paying extra every month and I didn't understand what was going on. I spent the first day panicking and asking everyone to pray for me. One of my friends suggested I ask our church for assistance. I was so afraid to do this. She said maybe God wants you to humble yourself and ask others for help. Still another friend said that maybe I should go to the government and seek assistance because of my health issues. Still another said that I should apply for a government subsidized apartment.

My first thought was, "God, please don't make me do that". I really didn't want to have to depend on the government for anything. Then I realized that I needed to give this to God and ask Him what He wanted me to do. In my spirit I felt God say that He controls the government, so He wasn't asking me to put my faith in anyone but Him. I had to get over myself and accept God's help in any way He wanted to help me. I realized I had often put limits on God, and expected Him to help me in exactly the way I decided that I needed to be helped. I also felt like He wanted me to go to our church and ask for assistance, which I did.

I started the process to apply for assistance from our church, and spent the next few days praying, fasting, and reading Scripture. I finally fell to my knees and told God that I didn't care where I lived as long as I was in His will. I thought that the worst that could happen would be we would end up living in the woods with other homeless people. I decided if we were lead to live in the woods with other homeless people, it was because God wanted to use that situation so that God could use us there to minister to others. I completely released my plan and asked God to reveal what He wanted me to do.

That night while Rick and I prayed before bed, God said to me that He was going to give me my place on the beach. I couldn't believe it! This couldn't be my imagination. I thought, well I don't know when this is going to happen, but if God told me then I believe it. I told Rick and he just laughed. I slept very well that night without worry, because I knew God had the plan.

The next morning when I woke up God directed me to Joel 2: 18-27. Verse 26 of the New Living Translation jumped off the page at me. It says, "Once again you will have all the food you want, and you will praise the Lord your God, who does these miracles for you. Never again will my people be disgraced." I realized He was saying that we would have even more than we needed and that we would finally be able to be a blessing to others.

I had always thought that it was selfish to ask for things. I thought I just needed to be thankful for just getting by. I don't believe that God wants us to be happy with mediocrity in our lives. I had been spending most of my life surviving it; thinking that Heaven was the only place that mattered. God was saying to me that I needed to start living abundantly here on this earth. Jesus died on the cross to save us from our sins, but also to give us the power to live victoriously in this life.

He also led me to Psalm 91, the whole chapter talks about God protecting us in our ways of obedience to him. When we love Him and trust Him, He gives His angels special charge over us to protect us. He also gave me Jeremiah 33:6, which says, "I will heal my people and will let them enjoy abundant peace and security." I instantly knew that everything was going to be okay. I didn't know what was going to happen, but I knew it would be for my ultimate good.

Shortly after my study and prayer time, I received a phone call from our landlord's realtor. He said that she had decided to work with us after all. We were not going to be evicted. I couldn't wait to tell the whole world what God had done for us.

After this experience, God continued to bring Joel 2:25 to my mind. I believed that this meant He was telling me He was going to repay me for all the years I had struggled. This was very exciting to me. I found myself speaking out words of encouragement everywhere I went. I had an unquenchable joy, which I couldn't explain. After all, our circumstances hadn't changed much. I still had no idea where the money to pay back the landlord was going to come from, but I knew that God would supply what we needed.

We were nearing the holidays again, and this had always been a stressful time for me. It always seemed we never had enough money to make ends meet, let alone, buy gifts for others. This holiday season was very different. I looked forward in anticipation to Thanksgiving and Christmas for the first time since I was a small child. Asia was scheduled to be home the day after Thanksgiving and I couldn't wait to see her again. I wanted to hear everything that God had been doing in her life and also share what God had been doing in my life.

When she came home she told me that God had called her to go back to YWAM to SOE (School of Evangelism). She was a little worried about the money needed, but having renewed faith I told her God was going to take care of that. I had been making a lot of jewelry while she was gone, and we started fundraising again.

Chapter 17

During the year, while working through my celebrate recovery Step Study I had received the forgiveness that Jesus died to give me. Having received His grace, God laid a desire on my heart for my family to be able to receive this same forgiveness and to be able to walk in grace and mercy. I had prayed many mornings just pleading with God for my mother and father to not just know that I had forgiven them, but that they were forgiven and to feel that forgiveness. I wanted them to know that they were free from the guilt and shame of all that had happened.

On Christmas Day, my father called me to wish me a happy birthday, and to tell me how much he loved me. He also told me how blessed he was, and that he didn't deserve it because he had done so much wrong in his life. I was able to remind him of the forgiveness we all have in Christ, and I could tell that he had truly received the forgiveness that I had pleaded with God for him to feel. God had given me an awesome birthday present and answered another prayer!

Asia was home in time for Christmas and her father had come down to visit with her. They both came over for

Christmas dinner. I felt so blessed that we could be together and celebrate Christ's birthday and also my own.

My sister, Toni, called to wish me a happy birthday. Her two children Daniel and Gabriella also got on the phone to talk to me. It touched my heart so deeply that they would want to talk to me, because I had been a stranger to them most of their lives.

My sister, Terri also called me as well. Then my foster family called. When I picked up the phone, they started to sing happy birthday. I just felt like this was the best birthday ever! I felt like God was restoring all I had lost in one day. I felt blessed beyond measure.

As the Step Study came to a close, I was a little sad. I knew that I would miss meeting with these wonderful women each week. Several of us were asked to share our testimony of what God had done for us through the study. I couldn't wait to share with others the healing I had received through this program.

I began to share with friends all the wonderful things that God was revealing to me. One day I was talking to a friend and jokingly said someday I'm going to write a book. She said, "Tammy you've been saying that for a long time. When are you going to write that book?" I realized she was right and I started asking God if He wanted me to write that book. Over the next few days I felt like He told me that He did want me to write a book to tell others what He had done for me and my family.

He also led me to co-facilitate a Step Study. He told me I needed to pour into others. I had heard that being a leader of a Step Study would have an even more powerful impact on me than going through the Step Study the first time. God reminded me again of the vision of Jesus and me driving down the road in the red convertible. I began waking up excited each day and couldn't wait to see what God was going to do next.

After the holidays we continued to work on fundraising for Asia's tuition. At the same time, I noticed that Rick's car needed tires and that the engine was making a strange noise. I knew we needed to take it into the shop, but we didn't have any extra money. All the extra income we had, we had given to the landlord. We also were trying to find a way to get Asia back to Texas for school. We kept checking the airfares, but there didn't seem to be any special deals.

One Sunday I was talking to a friend of mine at church and told her we needed new tires for the car. She told me that she had two brand new tires in her trunk. A friend had given her four, and she only needed two. I called Rick and we discovered that the tires were the size we needed. So we had two brand new tires for Rick's car. Then I needed to take the car to the shop. The next week we dropped the car off to have it looked at.

That morning the thought came to me that maybe I should take Asia to Texas in Rick's car. I wasn't sure if this was something from God, or just me wanting to take her. I asked her if she would mind if I drove her out there and she said that she loved that idea. She was much more excited about this trip to YWAM then she had been about the first one.

Our mechanic called later that day and said that the car needed a new serpentine belt and a new starter. He said the bill was $250, which was very inexpensive for the work he had done. However, we didn't have that much put aside. I was still trying to figure out how to come up with the gas money we needed to drive all the way to Texas from Southern Florida. We made arrangements to pay it off by the end of the week. I dropped Rick off to pick up the car at the end of the day. When he came home he asked me how much the car was supposed to cost. I thought maybe he was going to tell me that it was going to cost more than $250. He said that when he went to pick up the car that the bill had been paid in full anonymously by someone. I couldn't believe it. God had blessed us again. Asia, Rick and

I took this as confirmation that God wanted me to take Asia to YWAM. It seemed to me that He had fixed the car just in time for us to take the trip.

The week before Asia and I were scheduled to leave for Texas she still had not raised all the money she needed. One morning while I was praying, I felt like God told me that no matter how much money she had, we should get in the car and drive to Texas. He said "Trust Me". Asia and I were really struggling with trying to raise her tuition and I still didn't know where the gas money and money for a hotel was coming from. Asia came into my room the next morning to talk about what we were going to do. I told her that God had said that no matter how much money we had, we should get into the car and leave on Friday. A huge grin came over her face and she said that God had spoken the same thing to her, but she had been afraid to tell me. She said God told her that we had worked really hard to raise the money and now we should see what He could do. Again, this was a huge confirmation to me.

Later that morning one of my friends called me to tell me that she had a gift for me. She came to the house and handed me $120 in cash. She said she wished she could give me more. I told her that God had just answered my prayer for gas money for our trip. I had figured things out and thought I still had about $300 left in my checking account and decided that this should be just enough for our trip. We also had another friend give us $40, so I thought we would be able to make it. I still didn't have money for a hotel room, which worried Rick. I decided that God would give me the ability to drive straight through if I didn't have the money for a room. We stopped by a friend's house on our way out of town and it was then that I realized that I miscalculated what we had in our checking account. We only had forty dollars left in our checking account once our rent check cleared. A few checks had cleared that I had forgotten all about. I remember thinking, "Well, it's too late now and we're going." I kept this little fact to myself and just told God I trusted Him. I was terrified, but God had told us to go and we were going.

While we drove up the turnpike towards Texas, one of my friends called to tell me that I had a room reserved at the YWAM base for two nights for free with all meals provided. At that moment, I knew God had my back, I still didn't know how everything was going to work out, but I knew it would. Asia and I just couldn't believe all the miracles that were taking place. We drove straight through to Texas, making a few stops to eat along the way.

When we neared the YWAM ranch, it started to bring back memories of living in my foster home. The landscape was very similar to the area I had lived in as a child. I was so excited to see the place Asia had been spending so much of her time in. All of her friends ran to her and gave her warm hugs. I sat back and watched how she beamed, and I thought how wonderful it was to see her so happy. This was where she belonged; her home away from home. She was truly at home here and these people loved her. It warmed my heart to see that all the dreams I had wished for her were coming true.

I couldn't believe my eyes when I checked into my room. It was absolutely gorgeous! God had brought me to Texas in style. He had provided for me beyond my wildest expectations. It was so wonderful to crawl into the large comfortable bed and get a solid night's sleep after the long drive.

I awoke early in the morning and started to worry about how I was going to make it home. I certainly didn't have enough gas money to get home without bouncing our rent check. I couldn't believe how silly I was being. I felt just like the Israelites after seeing all the miracles God had performed to bring them out of Egypt and still they doubted. I kept telling myself, how could I tell Asia to trust God to bring her the money she needed to pay for her tuition and mission trip, and then not trust Him to provide what I needed to drive home? He had clearly told me to take this trip with her, and yet I was still struggling to believe that He would supply what I needed to make the journey home.

I realized I was really struggling with feeling worthy to have everything I needed provided. My low self-worth had plagued me all my life and still I was struggling even after He had told me I was the disciple whom He loved.

As I sat in my room that morning, I remembered how it felt when I first walked into the foster home. I realized that they welcomed me with open arms and I had been too far down in my pit of self-pity to appreciate them. God also told me that I had always looked at being removed from my family as a punishment, but this was a gift from Him. He had taken me out of the place that was not safe for me, and placed me into a loving, safe home. It broke my heart. I knew that I needed to call my foster mom and make amends to her for not appreciating her and all she had done for me.

It finally dawned on me why God had brought me on this journey. He wanted me to let go of the feeling that I had been punished all my life. He wanted me to be free to receive His love, and to stop looking at my life with the belief that it was ruined and beyond repair. God had always been with me and had been blessing me all my life. It was another turning point in my life. I told God once again that I believed, but help me with my unbelief.

I spent the rest of the weekend going between belief and unbelief. Every time a doubt came into my mind I just said, "God I trust you." I was scared to death, but I knew that God had not brought me out there to abandon me. He had the plan and it was my job to trust Him.

The night before I was supposed to leave for home a friend called me. She said that she needed me to pet sit for her the next month. She said she wanted to pay me in advance. The total cost for the pet sitting was $250 and it was enough to enable me to drive home. One of Asia's friends asked me if I had a place to stay over on the way home. I said that I wasn't sure. She said that her cousin, Rachel, would be happy to let me stay in her home on the way home. Again God was chasing me down with blessing. He was giving me more than I needed. I couldn't wait to get home and share with everyone how God had supplied all my needs in abundance.

I left for home on Monday morning. One of the first calls I made on the way home was to my foster mom. I asked her to forgive me for not allowing her to truly come into my heart. I told her I was sorry for how I had treated her. I told her how blessed I was to have her to take care of me during that difficult time. She in turn told me that I was such a blessing to her, and we cried healing tears with each other.

I drove throughout the day talking to God and thanking Him for everything He had done. By early evening I had arrived in Pace, Florida at Rachel's home. She and her husband graciously welcomed me into their home. They gave me dinner and had already made my bed. I was able to take a shower and go to bed. I had never been welcomed into a stranger's home before and I was so blessed. In the morning Rachel and I were able to fellowship with each other for a few hours. We were able to encourage each other. I left for home in the late morning, refreshed and ready for the last eight hours of the drive home.

When I returned home I had a clear vision of the testimony God wanted me to write. The next morning I woke up with an enormous amount of information for my testimony. I was overwhelmed by it all and then one of my friends reminded me that some of this information was also for the book that God had told me to write. I had my testimony written by the end of the week. I was excited to share it with others.

Everyone kept asking me if I was nervous during the weeks leading up to the night of my testimony. I really wasn't, but thought I would be when I finally got up in front of all those people. Finally the night of my testimony arrived. I had invited several people and quite a few came. My sponsor gave a beautiful introduction and I walked up on the stage. To my surprise, I wasn't nervous at all. I realized that God had given me the words to say and He was using me to touch the people He wanted to reach. Afterward, several people came up and thanked me for sharing my testimony. I realized that God had touched lives through me sharing my life story and the healing I had received from Him. It was then that I decided that I wanted God to use me to have an impact on as many people as possible. I couldn't wait to see what God had in store for me. A far cry from the woman who thought God was waiting for her to mess up so He could punish her. What a difference a change in our perspective can make.

Epilogue

The journey God has taken me on has taught me many things, now that I finally decided to allow Him to have control. I now know I'm not perfect and I'm not going to be here on this earth, but God does amazing things through imperfect human beings. He has also taught me that in order to receive His abundant power in addition to giving Him complete control; I need to trust Him completely no matter how I feel or what my circumstances are.

Today, I have much more of God's peace, joy, and love. I'm excited to get up every morning to see what God's going to do today. I'm excited to know that this is just the beginning of my journey with God. In short, I have my passion for life back!

With God's help I have started to impact people around me in positive ways. He has developed me to be an encourager and to see the good in others, even when they can't see it themselves. He is developing me to be a strong prayer warrior. I have been able to trust Him with my finances like never before. People around me have shared with me how different I seem. They've told me I seem happy and peaceful something that is very new to me.

God has begun to transform the relationships I have with my family. Through Celebrate Recovery God has restored my relationship with my biological family as well as my foster family. God reminded me recently of all the things I thought I'd lost, and how He is restoring them to me, better than they were to begin with. Joel 2:25 says, "I will repay you for all the years the locusts have eaten…" I have begun to have a real relationship with my sisters, and have become an aunt to a wonderful nephew and niece. My daughter is building her own life with God, and we have a new, more wonderful relationship. My husband and I are continuing to grow our marriage. I am also blessed to see many of the generational curses of my family broken and know that we are now truly set free. God continues to amaze me daily; the blessings just keep flowing.

I won't tell you that I no longer struggle with pride, fear, unbelief, anger or any other defect of character. I struggle every day, but I choose to hand over my struggles and surrender to God far more quickly than ever before. I also have people that God has place around me that I can reach out to that will listen without judging and pray with me. In the words of Joyce Meyer, "I'm not where I need to be, but thank God, I'm not where I used to be."

About the Author

Author Tammy Schaefer is first and foremost a child of God, a wife and mother who moved to Stuart, FL in 2009 from Lancaster, Pennsylvania after her husband became unemployed. God brought her through abuse, self-loathing and into healing by revealing His fierce love for her. After showing her His great love, He brought back the vision He had planted in her at an early age and is working with her to make it even bigger that she ever imagined. Her husband Rick is her best friend, supporting her in her dreams. Her daughter, Asia is her hero and has taught her mother many things about walking by faith. Asia is currently serving God in YWAM (Youth With A Mission), sharing God's love in practical ways in the U.S. and around the world. Tammy feels truly blessed to live in Florida as this was one of her dreams from the time she was a young child. She is self-employed as a resume writer and a pet sitter part-time and is currently serving as a co-facilitator in a Celebrate Recovery step study. She's been blessed with the gift of encouragement and enjoys helping others see the natural gifts and talents that God has blessed them with. She recently has come to understand what it means to be completely loved and accepted by God and wants others to experience this amazing love for themselves. Currently

Tammy is working on the second of many inspirational books she feels led to write. She has a dream to bring a healing ministry to her local church to empower others to become mighty warriors for God and enable them to travel throughout the world with God's message of love. It brings her great joy to see others receive God's love and embrace the greatness He created them for.

63056996R00083

Made in the USA
Charleston, SC
27 October 2016